CAKE CRAFT

MADE EASY

CAKE CRAFT
MADE EASY

Step-by-Step Sugarcraft Techniques
for 16 Vintage-Inspired Cakes

≈Fiona Pearce≈

David and Charles

www.stitchcraftcreate.co.uk

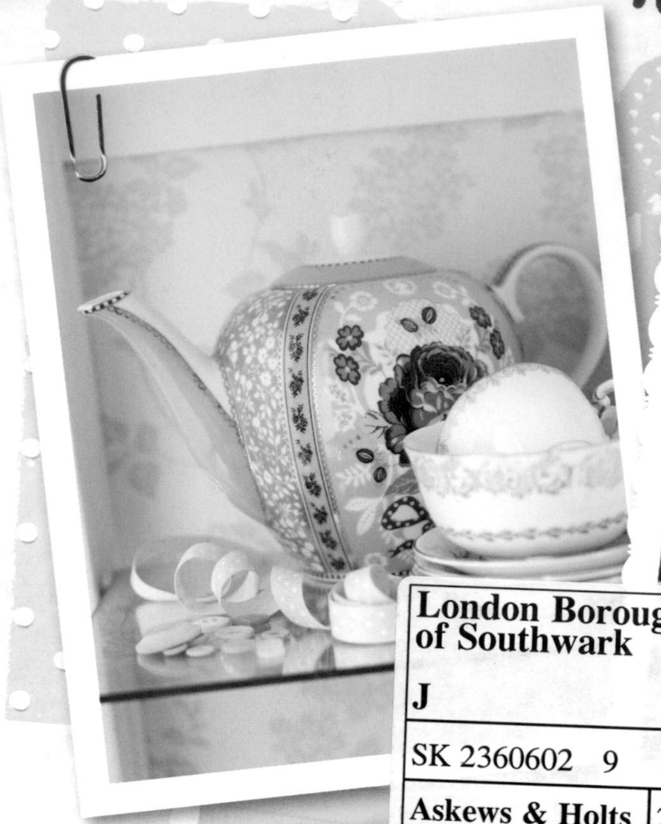

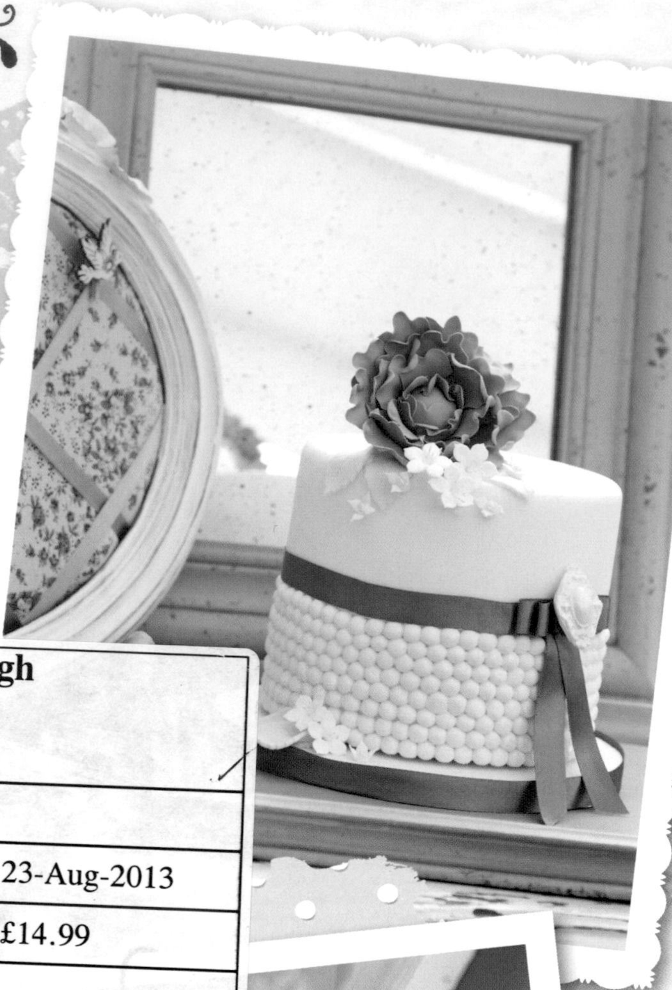

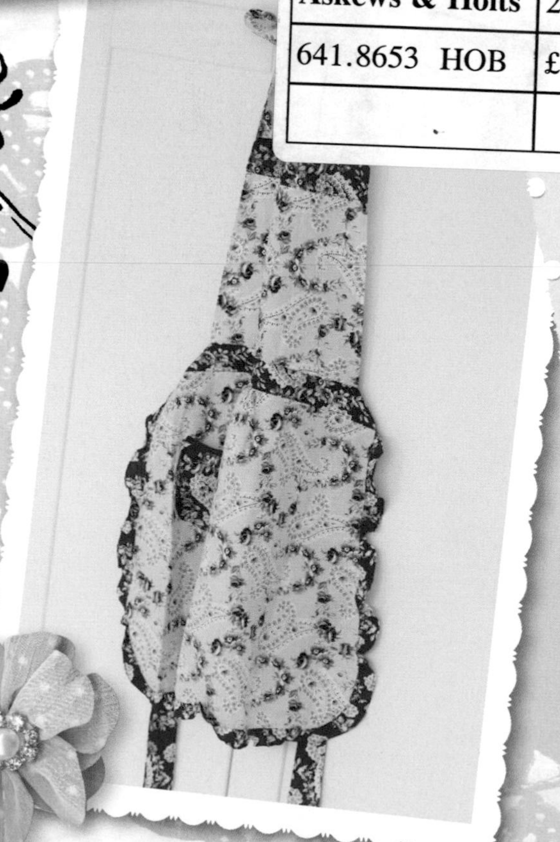

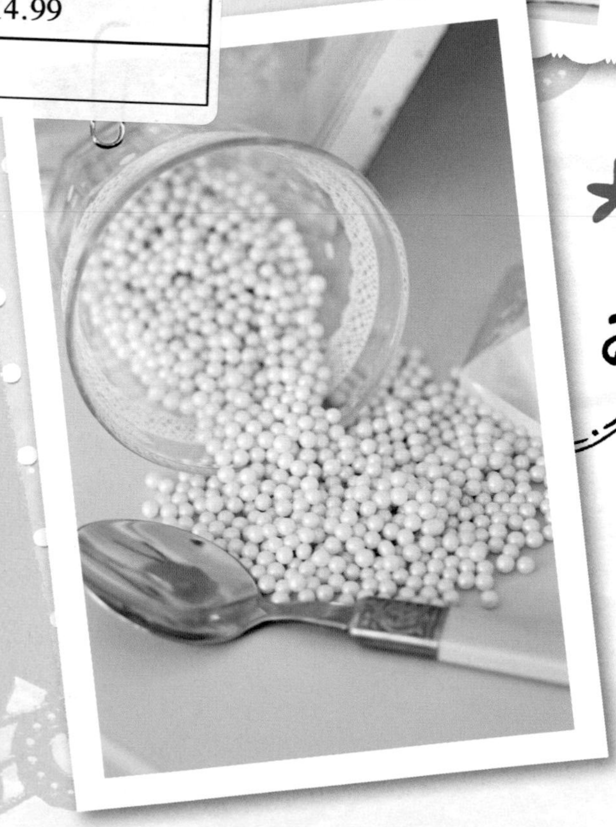

Contents

Introduction

Welcome to *Cake Craft Made Easy*.

Since I began posting online cake decorating tutorials on my blog Icing Bliss and teaching cake decorating classes, I realized that many people falsely believe that pretty cake decorations are beyond their ability. However, in truth, with a little practice and a few cake decorating tools, beautiful creations are not out of anyone's reach.

This book features 12 projects, each with detailed step-by-step instructions to assist readers in mastering simple cake decorating techniques and create impressive single-tier cakes for all occasions. Each project demonstrates how to prepare a cake before decorations can be added and features different techniques including using royal icing for stencilling and brush embroidery, creating simple patterns with buttercream and making beautiful flowers and decorations with flower (petal/gum) paste. I have chosen the designs to suit beginners who have little or no previous cake decorating experience, but I hope this book will also serve to inspire more experienced cake decorators and act as a design resource. The projects are ordered to include simple techniques in earlier chapters and techniques that involve more complex steps in the later sections of the book.

While the instructions for each project will enable you to reproduce every one of the cakes exactly, I encourage you to adapt the designs and experiment with colours to make your creations unique. If you take the time to also make a few extra decorations while completing each project, you will quickly build up a useful collection of attractive decorations that you can use another day on other bakes such as cookies or cupcakes.

Although I have included some staple recipes, this book was intended to focus on sugarcraft rather than baking. Acknowledging that a lot

of people don't have the time or the patience to bake cakes and just want to focus on decorating, there is no shame in using store-bought sponges or plain cakes from supermarkets for these projects.

I hope that you enjoy the projects in this book and will feel inspired to use the techniques learned in your future cake endeavours.

Happy Cake Crafting!

Toolbox

There is an endless amount of kitchen utensils and cake decorating tools available to buy, but here are a few items that are regularly used throughout this book and will be useful for any future cake decorating projects.

Basic Cake Craft Kit

Cake leveller for cutting uniform layers of cake

Cake smoothers for achieving a smooth finish on sugarpaste (rolled fondant)-covered cakes and boards

Cake turntable to easily turn a cake as you are decorating it

Edible glue for attaching decorations to cakes

Large and small knives for cutting sugarpaste

Large and small non-stick rolling pins for rolling out sugarpaste and flower (petal/gum) paste

Large non-stick board on which to roll out pastes

Paintbrushes (range of thicknesses) for dusting and gluing decorations and for brush embroidery

Serrated knife for cutting cakes to size

Spatulas or palette knives for applying fillings and 'crumb coating' cakes

Spoons (teaspoons, tablespoons) for mixing icing, filling piping (pastry) bags and for drying petals in curved shapes

Creative Tools

Ball tool for shaping decorations

Bone tool for frilling the edges of flower (petal/gum) paste decorations

Cake board on which to present the cake

Cake card as a template to cut out specific cake shapes and sizes, and for attaching to the base of miniature cakes (or cupcake towers)

Cocktail sticks (toothpicks) for adding colour to icing and for frilling flower paste

Cookie cutters to cut cookie dough into different shapes

Double-sided tape for attaching ribbons to cakes and cake boards

Edible icing sheet printed with a design that can be cut out and used on cookies or to make cake decorations

Edible lustre dust to add sparkle to decorations and cakes

Edible pearls for decorating cakes and cupcakes

Embossing stamps for adding patterns or texture to sugarpaste (rolled fondant)

5-petal rose cutters for making layered flowers or roses

Florist wire to support sugar flowers and to attach to decorations to make them stand up out of the cake

Foam pad used to cushion decorations as they are being shaped and frilled

Garrett frill cutter for cutting out ruffles

Metal ruler for measuring cakes, guiding the cutting of even strips of sugarpaste and ensuring even spacing between decorations on cakes

Paint palette for mixing edible paints and dusts, and shaping decorations

Paste food colouring to colour icing

Patchwork cutters for cutting out decorations or embossing sugarpaste

Piping (pastry) bags to fill with buttercream or royal icing

Piping tubes (tips) for piping royal icing and buttercream

Pizza cutter for cutting out strips of sugarpaste or flower paste to make bows and ribbon roses

Plunger cutters for making decorations in sugarpaste and flower paste such as leaves, hearts and blossoms

Posy pick to hold wired decorations in a cake

Quilting tool to emboss sugarpaste with a stitching effect

Rice (wafer) paper to make edible, translucent decorations such as flowers

Scissors to cut out flower paste, edible icing sheets and rice paper

Scribing tool for marking designs into cakes or adding texture to sugarpaste

Shaped cutters (metal and plastic varieties) for cutting out shapes in sugarpaste and flower paste such as leaves, petals, flowers and geometric shapes

Silicone moulds for making decorations in sugarpaste or flower paste such as buttons, brooches and pearls

Spacers for rolling out sugarpaste or dough to an even thickness

Squeezy bottle filled with thinned royal icing to flood (cover) a cookie

Stencils to add patterns to cakes with edible lustre dusts or royal icing

Tweezers for adding edible pearls and dragées (sugar balls) to cakes and decorations

Vellum paper for wrapping around cakes to add a pattern

Vintage Chic Cupcake Towers

This is a quick and creative take on those miniature cakes you often see at weddings and on dessert tables. Here instead, cupcakes are stacked on top of each other with buttercream and covered in sugarpaste to make lovely little towers, which can be clustered together or arranged on tiered stands for formal occasions, or individually wrapped in cellophane as a gift.

TECHNIQUE CHECKLIST *In this project you will learn how to:*

- ✓ Cut, fill, stack and 'crumb coat' cupcakes to make a tower

- ✓ Cover cupcake towers with sugarpaste (rolled fondant)

- ✓ Use flower (petal/gum) paste to make ribbon roses, bows, rosettes and a strand of pearls

- ✓ Use edible pearls and vellum paper to prettify the towers

YOU WILL NEED

- 6 large (muffin-sized) cupcakes or 9 small cupcakes (fairy cakes)

- 250g (9oz) buttercream

- 500g (1lb 2oz) pale grey sugarpaste (rolled fondant)

- flower (petal/gum) paste: 50g (1¾oz) each white and pale pink

- 1 tbsp royal icing in a piping (pastry) bag fitted with a no. 2 round piping tube (tip)

- edible pearls

- metal circle cutters: same diameter as the base of the cupcakes, and 5cm (2in)

- three 7.5cm (3in) round cake cards

- ribbon (plus optional lace) and double-sided tape

- vellum paper (I used a lace pattern)

- pearl necklace silicone mould (First Impressions)

- pizza cutter (optional)

- scissors and tweezers

- Basic Cake Craft Kit (see Toolbox)

Preparing the cupcake towers

1 Take 2 large or 3 small cupcakes that have been frozen for 15 minutes after baking, unwrap from their paper cases (liners) and turn them upside down on a board. Level the tops with a sharp knife.

2 Use the circle cutter the same diameter as the base of the cupcakes to trim the edge of each cupcake away so that you are left with even cylindrical-shaped cakes of the same size (A).

3 Using a spatula or palette knife, add buttercream to the top of each cupcake and then stack 2 large (or 3 small) cupcakes on each other to make a tower (B). If any buttercream squishes out from the joins, just spread it around the outside of the tower with the spatula. Repeat this process to make 3 towers.

4 The next stage is to 'crumb coat' the towers to hold the crumbs of cake in place. Spread a thin layer of buttercream on the side and top of each tower with a spatula (C). It is easiest to add more buttercream than you need to start with and then scrape off any excess once it has been applied evenly to the whole tower. Aim to spread the buttercream over the tower so that it is thin enough for the crumbs show through.

5 Attach each tower to a cake card with a small amount of buttercream and then chill them for about 30 minutes in the fridge until the buttercream is firm.

6 Once the crumb coat has set, knead the grey sugarpaste well until it is soft and pliable. Using a large non-stick rolling pin, roll out the sugarpaste into a rough circle shape on a non-stick board until it is approximately 5mm (³⁄₁₆in) thick. Lift the sugarpaste off the board with the rolling pin and lay it gently over one cupcake tower (D).

D

7 Use your hands to smooth the paste over the top and down the side of the tower. As the sugarpaste is smoothed down the side, you may find that it starts to form pleats towards the base of the tower. If so, gently lift the sugarpaste away from the side of the tower and smooth it down again so that it lays flat against the tower (E). Don't smooth over the top of pleats, otherwise it will leave creases in your sugarpaste.

E

8 Trim off any excess sugarpaste from around the base of the tower with a small sharp knife (F).

9 Use a smoother – preferably 2 if you have them – to polish the top and side of the tower (G). This will press out any air bubbles that may be trapped under the sugarpaste and will give your tower a nice smooth finish. Repeat steps 6–9 to cover the remaining 2 towers.

F

10 Attach a ribbon around the base of 2 towers with double-sided tape. For the third tower, cut out a strip of vellum paper and wrap it around the tower so that it covers the bottom two-thirds. Secure the paper in place with double-sided tape. Tie a lace ribbon around the centre of the vellum paper if desired.

G

Bow

1 Knead the white flower paste until it is soft and pliable. Using a non-stick rolling pin, roll out the paste thinly on a non-stick board and trim it with a sharp knife or pizza cutter into a strip approximately 3cm (1¼in) wide and 12cm (4¾in) long.

2 Pinch the centre of the strip together and apply edible glue to the top of the pinched section with a fine paintbrush (**A**).

3 Pleat each end of the strip and then fold them one at a time in towards the centre, securing them onto the edible glue (**B–C**).

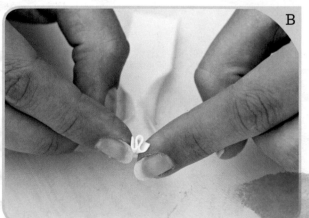

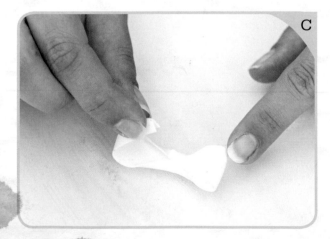

4 Cut out a small strip of white flower paste approximately 2cm (¾in) wide and 5cm (2in) long. Apply edible glue to the back of the strip (D). Place the centre of the strip (glue-side down) over the top of the centre of the bow and secure the ends of the strip on the underside of the bow (E).

5 To make the tails for the bow, roll out some white flower paste and cut out 2 strips approximately 2.5cm (1in) wide. You can make the tails as long as you like – I cut mine to 8cm (3¼in).

6 Using a small knife, cut an arrowhead into one end of each tail (F).

7 Stick the tails on top of the tower with edible glue so that they gently drape over the edge (G). Attach the bow on top with royal icing (H).

Tip

Plump up the loops of the bow by adding kitchen paper (paper towel) inside them while drying.

D

E

F

G

H

Ribbon rose

1 Using a non-stick rolling pin, roll out a strip of pink flower paste thinly. The longer you roll out your strip, the bigger your ribbon rose will be. To make a small rose, aim to make a strip that is at least 15cm (6in) long and 3cm (1¼in) wide.

2 Starting at either end of the strip, begin to roll it up like a snail shell. This will form the centre of your ribbon rose.

3 Begin to wrap the strip around the centre of the rose, pinching the paste into pleats at the base of the rose as you go along to give it a ruffle effect.

4 Once the rose is the size you require, trim off the remaining part of the strip (if any) with scissors. Your ribbon rose will have a long ugly tail at this stage. Don't worry – just trim it off with a knife or scissors.

5 Attach the ribbon rose to the cupcake towers with royal icing. I have added a ribbon rose to the tower with the bow and also on the side of the tower wrapped in vellum paper.

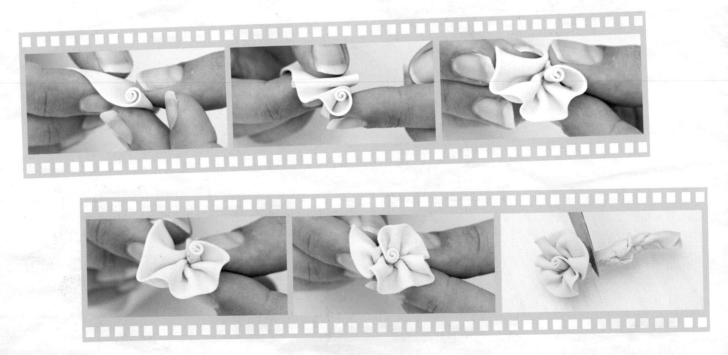

Decorating with edible pearls

I have added edible pearls in the shape of a heart to the top of the tower that is wrapped in vellum paper. I have also added a few to the tower that features the bow and ribbon rose.

Using a pair of tweezers, press edible pearls, one at a time, into the cupcake tower to create a pattern (A). It is important that this is done while the sugarpaste covering is still soft, otherwise the sugarpaste will crack. If the paste is fresh, it will be sticky enough to hold the pearls in place.

A

Tip

If the edible pearls do pop out of the sugarpaste, you can secure them back in place with edible glue.

Strand of pearls

1 Knead the white flower paste until it is soft and pliable. Roll into a thin sausage approximately the length and width of the pearl necklace mould you would like to use.

2 Starting at one end of the mould, press the flower paste firmly along the length of the mould. Don't worry if it overfills the mould — just use a knife to trim off the excess paste.

3 Flex the mould to remove the pearl strand (A). Drape the strand over the top and edge of the cupcake tower and attach in place using edible glue applied with a fine paintbrush.

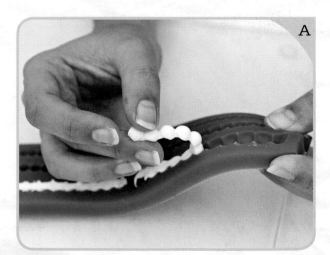

A

Rosette

1 Knead the white flower paste until it is soft and pliable. Using a non-stick rolling pin, roll out the paste thinly. Use the 5cm (2in) circle cutter to cut out a circle (**A**).

2 Roll out 2 strips of white and pink flower paste approximately 2cm (¾in) wide. Using edible glue, attach the pink strip, gathering the paste into a ruffle as you go along, to the outside edge of the white circle (**B**).

3 To complete the rosette, add more edible glue to the inside section of the circle (**C**) and repeat step 2 but using the white strip this time to fill the circle. Don't worry if you can still see the white centre.

A

B

C

4 Pipe royal icing into the centre of the rosette (D) and use tweezers to affix edible pearls in place (E). You can add as many edible pearls as you like!

5 Leave the rosette to dry for at least an hour before attaching it to the top of the cupcake tower with royal icing – I have added it to the one that features the pearl strand.

Tip

Make the ribbon roses and rosette in advance and keep them in a container at room temperature away from moisture.

D

E

Focus on... HOW TO MAKE A RIBBON ROSE

Go to

http://ideas.stitchcraftcreate.co.uk/
kitchen/videos/

for a video tutorial on how to make a ribbon rose using flower paste.

~ Vintage Chic Cupcake Towers ~

Trio of Buttercream Beauties

This fun collection of pastel-coloured cakes piped with buttercream designs is perfect to share with friends. If you don't want to make all three, you can choose just one or two of the designs. While the piping techniques in this project are easy to achieve, it's always a good idea to practise piping onto an upturned cake tin before decorating the cakes.

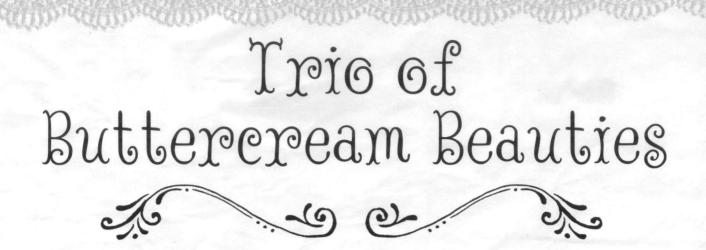

TECHNIQUE CHECKLIST In this project you will learn how to...

✓ Stack, fill and 'crumb coat' a round cake with buttercream

✓ Use buttercream to pipe pretty strips of ribbon, scallops and ruffles onto a cake

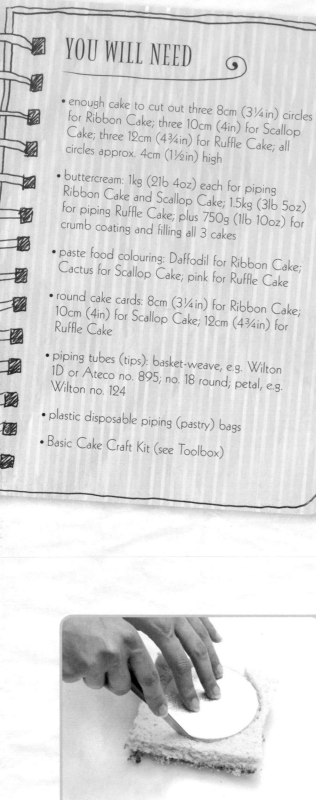

YOU WILL NEED

- enough cake to cut out three 8cm (3¼in) circles for Ribbon Cake; three 10cm (4in) for Scallop Cake; three 12cm (4¾in) for Ruffle Cake; all circles approx. 4cm (1½in) high

- buttercream: 1kg (2lb 4oz) each for piping Ribbon Cake and Scallop Cake; 1.5kg (3lb 5oz) for piping Ruffle Cake; plus 750g (1lb 10oz) for crumb coating and filling all 3 cakes

- paste food colouring: Daffodil for Ribbon Cake; Cactus for Scallop Cake; pink for Ruffle Cake

- round cake cards: 8cm (3¼in) for Ribbon Cake; 10cm (4in) for Scallop Cake; 12cm (4¾in) for Ruffle Cake

- piping tubes (tips): basket-weave, e.g. Wilton 1D or Ateco no. 895; no. 18 round; petal, e.g. Wilton no. 124

- plastic disposable piping (pastry) bags

- Basic Cake Craft Kit (see Toolbox)

Preparing the cakes

1 Trim the crust off the cake with a serrated knife (A).

2 Place one of the cake cards on top of the cake and cut around the card with a small sharp knife, being careful to hold the knife straight and not at an angle (B). Repeat to cut out 3 circles of cake for each size of cake card (9 circles of cake in total).

3 If the circles of cake are not even in height, gently pull a cake leveller through each one to make them uniform (C).

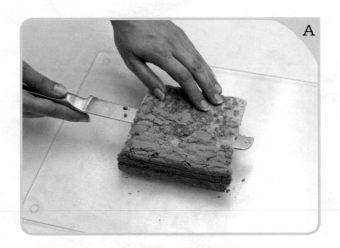

A

B

C

4 Place one circle of cake on top of its corresponding cake card, using a little of the buttercream to hold it in place. Use a spatula or palette knife to spread buttercream evenly on top of the cake. Add the next layer of cake on top and spread with buttercream as before (D), then top with the final cake layer. Repeat to assemble the other 2 cakes.

5 The next stage is to 'crumb coat' the cakes to hold the crumbs of cake in place. First, spread buttercream over the sides of the cakes with the spatula (E).

6 Then spread buttercream over the top of the cake (F). It's easiest to add more buttercream than you need to start with and then scrape off any excess once it has been applied evenly to the whole cake. Aim to spread the buttercream so that it is thin enough for the crumbs to show through.

7 Place the cakes in the fridge until the crumb coat has set (usually about 1 hour). This will make the cakes firm so that it is easier to apply the buttercream piping (G).

Tip

Add a little cooled boiled water to the buttercream to make it easier to spread.

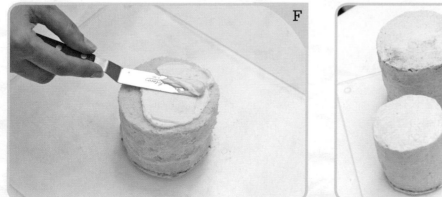

Trio of Buttercream Beauties

Ribbon cake

1 While the cakes are firming in the fridge, use the Daffodil paste food colouring to colour the buttercream for piping this cake pale yellow. Fit a disposable piping bag with the basket-weave piping tube and spoon in the buttercream.

2 Once firm, place the 8cm (3¼in) cake on a sturdy board on top of a cake turntable. Position the piping tube at the base of the cake so that the slit in the tube is horizontal, with the smooth edge of the slit touching the board and the jagged edge on top. Pipe a straight ribbon of buttercream vertically up the side of the cake (A). Don't worry if you pipe the ribbon slightly over the top of the cake; you will be able to smooth it onto the top of the cake later.

3 Pipe the next ribbon as in step 2 but position the piping tube halfway overlapping the first ribbon before piping (B). Continue to pipe ribbons in this manner, turning the cake turntable as you go, until the entire side of the cake is covered.

4 Use a palette knife or spatula to smooth the top of the ribbons over the top of the cake. Add some more buttercream to the top of the cake and smooth it out to cover the rest of the top of the cake so that no cake crumbs can be seen (C).

Tip

If the buttercream becomes too soft while you are piping, put it back in the fridge for a few minutes. The piped designs will not look as clean if the buttercream is too soft.

Scallop cake

1 While the cakes are firming in the fridge, use the Cactus paste food colouring to colour the buttercream for piping this cake pale green. Fit a disposable piping bag with the no. 18 round piping tube and spoon in the buttercream.

2 Once set, place the 10cm (4in) cake on a board on top of the cake turntable. Position the piping tube at the base of the cake and then pipe 8 dots of buttercream in a vertical line up the side of the cake, each immediately above the other (A).

3 To achieve the scallop effect, use the end of a teaspoon or the piping tube to smear the dots of buttercream to the right (B). It is best to wipe the teaspoon or piping tube clean after you have smeared 3 dots.

4 Start piping the next line of dots over part of the smeared section of the previous dots, and smear into the scallop shape (C). Continue to pipe the scallops, turning the turntable as you go, until the side of the cake is completely covered.

5 Pipe scallops on the top of the cake as in step 3 (D). Start on the outside edge of the cake and gradually work around in a spiral formation until you reach the centre.

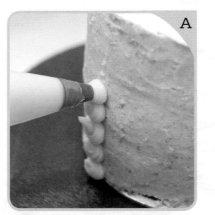

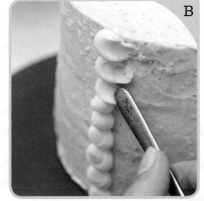

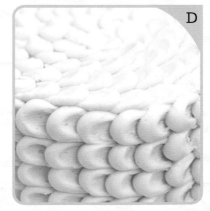

Ruffle cake

1 While the cakes are firming in the fridge, use the pink paste food colouring to colour the buttercream for piping this cake peach. Fit a disposable piping bag with the petal piping tube and spoon in the buttercream.

2 Once set, place the 12cm (4¾in) cake on a sturdy board on top of the cake turntable. You will notice that the tip of the piping tube is shaped as a teardrop with a broad end and a narrow end (**A**). When piping, the broad end should be touching the cake and the narrow end facing you, otherwise the ruffles will be chunky!

3 Holding the piping bag at a 45-degree angle to the cake, position the piping tube perpendicular to the base of the cake and then slowly squeeze out the buttercream while moving the piping bag right and left quickly as you gently move vertically up the side of the cake to the top, until you have piped a strip of ruffles (**B**).

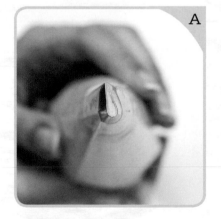

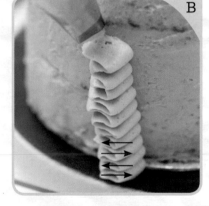

4 Continue piping vertical strips of ruffles next to each other until the side of your cake is completely covered (**C**).

5 For the top of the cake, hold the piping bag so that the narrow end of the piping tube is pointing away from the centre of the cake. Pipe ruffles by moving the piping bag backwards and forwards while squeezing, starting on the outside edge of the cake (**D**).

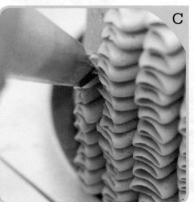

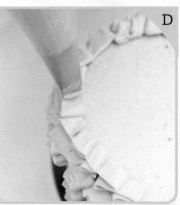

6 Continue to pipe ruffles around the outside of the cake, gradually working inwards in a spiral formation until you reach the centre (E).

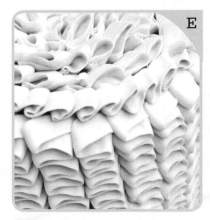

Tip

Use the petal tip to pipe ruffles onto cupcakes to accompany your cake.

Focus on... HOW TO PIPE BUTTERCREAM RUFFLES

Go to
http://ideas.stitchcraftcreate.co.uk/ kitchen/videos/
for a quick tutorial on how to use buttercream to pipe ruffles onto a cake.

ᐳ Trio of Buttercream Beauties ᐸ

Dreamy Dahlia

Although not as widespread as sugarpaste in cake decorating, rice paper is a highly versatile medium that can be used to make enchanting delicate decorations, as in this project where petals are hand-crafted from rice paper and then assembled in a circular pattern to create a dahlia. If pressed for time, you can simply modify the cake design and make smaller blooms.

TECHNIQUE CHECKLIST *In this project you will learn how to*

✓ Stack, fill and 'crumb coat' a square cake with buttercream

✓ Cover a square cake with sugarpaste (rolled fondant)

✓ Make a large dahlia flower using rice (wafer) paper

YOU WILL NEED

- enough cake to cut out three 15cm (6in) squares approx. 5cm (2in) high
- 600g (1lb 5oz) buttercream
- 1kg (2lb 4oz) purple sugarpaste (rolled fondant)
- 1 tbsp royal icing in a piping (pastry) bag fitted with a no. 2 round piping tube (tip)
- 10g (¼oz) white flower (petal/gum) paste
- edible gold lustre dust
- A4 sheet of white (uncoloured) rice paper or edible wafer paper
- 15cm (6in) square cake card
- 15cm (6in) square cake board
- ribbon (at least 70cm/27½in long) and double-sided tape
- 9.5cm (3¾in) metal circle cutter
- thick dusting brush (a new blusher brush works well)
- scissors
- Basic Cake Craft Kit (see Toolbox)

Preparing the cake

1 Trim the crust off the cake with a serrated knife. Place the square cake card on top of the cake and cut around the card, being careful to hold your knife straight and not at an angle (A). Repeat to cut out 3 squares of cake. If the squares are not even in height, gently pull a cake leveller through each one to make them uniform (B).

2 Use a spatula or palette knife to spread the buttercream evenly onto the first layer of cake. Try not to add too much, otherwise it will ooze out of the side of the cake. Add the next layer of cake on top and spread with buttercream as before (C), then top with the final layer of cake.

A

B

C

Dreamy Dahlia

30

3 The next stage is to 'crumb coat' the cake to hold the crumbs of cake in place. Spread buttercream over the sides and top of the cake with the spatula. Aim to spread the buttercream over the cake so that it is thin enough for the crumbs to show through.

4 Place the cake in the fridge until the crumb coat has set (about 1 hour). This will make the cake firm so that it is easier to apply the sugarpaste covering.

5 Once the crumb coat has set, knead the purple sugarpaste well until it is soft and pliable. Using a large non-stick rolling pin, roll out the sugarpaste into a rough square shape on a non-stick board until it is approximately 5mm (³⁄₁₆in) thick. Lift the sugarpaste off the board with the rolling pin and lay it gently over the cake (**D**).

6 Use your hands to smooth the sugarpaste over the top and down the corners of the cake. Try to work as quickly as possible to make sure that the sugarpaste doesn't tear on the edges or corners of the cake.

7 Next, use your hands to smooth the sugarpaste over the sides of the cake. As the sugarpaste is smoothed down the sides, you may find that it starts to form pleats towards the base of the cake. If so, gently lift the sugarpaste away from the side of the cake and smooth it down so that it lays flat against the cake. Don't smooth over the top of pleats, otherwise it will leave creases in your sugarpaste.

8 Trim off any excess sugarpaste from around the base of the cake with a small sharp knife (**E**).

9 Use a smoother — preferably 2 if you have them — to polish the top and sides. This will help press out any air bubbles that may be trapped under the sugarpaste and will give your cake a nice smooth finish.

10 Attach the cake to the cake board with royal icing. Trim the base of the cake and cake board with ribbon, securing it with double-sided tape.

11 Tip a small amount of edible gold lustre dust onto a sheet of kitchen paper (paper towel), then dab the thick dusting brush into the dust to load it with colour. Apply to the surface of the cake using gentle brush strokes (**F**).

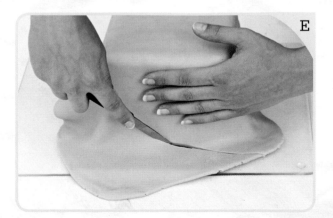

☞ Dreamy Dahlia ☜

Rice paper dahlia

1 Using a non-stick rolling pin, roll out the white flower paste on a non-stick board. Press the circle cutter firmly into the paste to cut out a large circle (**A**). Leave the circle to one side while you are preparing the petals.

2 Using a small sharp knife or scissors and a metal ruler, cut the rice paper into strips approximately 2cm (¾in) wide (**B**).

3 Next, cut each strip into 10 squares with scissors (**C**).

4 Then use the scissors to round one side of each square into a petal shape (**D**). You will need approximately 150 petals in total.

5 Apply a very small amount of water to the straight edge of each rice paper petal with a fine paintbrush. Be careful not to add too much water, otherwise the rice paper will disintegrate (**E**).

6 Fold the straight sides of the petal into the centre — the wet edge of the petal should hold them in place (**F**).

7 Once you have made all of the petals, apply a small amount of water to the flower paste circle with a paintbrush and stick the petals down side by side, starting from the outer edge of the circle (**G**).

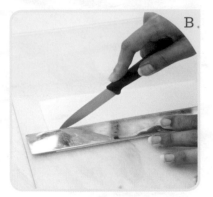

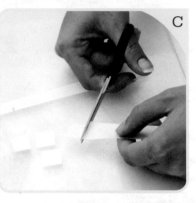

Tip

Rice paper is also available in various colours if you want to make different-coloured flowers to suit your occasion, or spray uncoloured rice paper with edible lustre sprays.

⌐ Dreamy Dahlia ⌐

8 Continue to add petals to the inside section of the circle, slightly overlapping the previous rows, until you reach the centre and the entire base is covered.

9 Attach the dahlia to the centre of the front of the cake with royal icing.

Tip

Make smaller dahlias by using 25 petals on a flower paste circle 3.5cm (1⅜in) in diameter and place on top of cupcakes to complement your cake.

Focus on... HOW TO MAKE A RICE PAPER DAHLIA

Go to

http://ideas.stitchcraftcreate.co.uk/ kitchen/videos/

for a video tutorial on how to make a dahlia flower with rice paper.

◞ Dreamy Dahlia ◟

Baked with Love

As an alternative to sugarpaste decorations, cookies can be decorated with royal icing and attached around the edge of a cake. Although some people find piping patterns with royal icing quite daunting, by practising on cookies you will become proficient in simple royal icing techniques in no time!

TECHNIQUE CHECKLIST In this project you will learn how to......

✓ Stack, fill and 'crumb coat' a round cake with chocolate ganache

✓ Use royal icing to flood (cover) heart-shaped cookies

✓ Pipe a polka dot pattern with royal icing

YOU WILL NEED

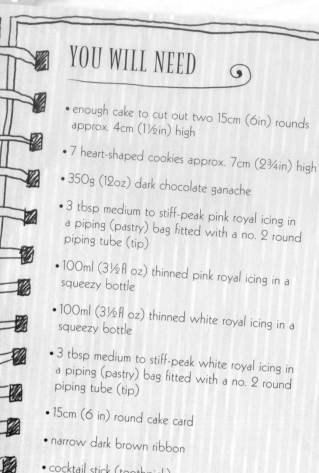

- enough cake to cut out two 15cm (6in) rounds approx. 4cm (1½in) high

- 7 heart-shaped cookies approx. 7cm (2¾in) high

- 350g (12oz) dark chocolate ganache

- 3 tbsp medium to stiff-peak pink royal icing in a piping (pastry) bag fitted with a no. 2 round piping tube (tip)

- 100ml (3½ fl oz) thinned pink royal icing in a squeezy bottle

- 100ml (3½ fl oz) thinned white royal icing in a squeezy bottle

- 3 tbsp medium to stiff-peak white royal icing in a piping (pastry) bag fitted with a no. 2 round piping tube (tip)

- 15cm (6 in) round cake card

- narrow dark brown ribbon

- cocktail stick (toothpick)

- pin (optional)

- Basic Cake Craft Kit (see Toolbox)

Tip

If possible, allow ganache to rest at room temperature overnight before using it. This will ensure that it can be spread smoothly onto the cake without tearing it.

Preparing the cake

1 Trim the crust off the cake with a serrated knife. Place the round cake card on top of the cake and cut around the card, being careful to hold your knife straight and not at an angle (A). Repeat to cut out 2 rounds of cake. If the rounds are not even in height, gently pull a cake leveller through each one to make them uniform.

2 Attach the first layer of cake to the cake card with a small amount of ganache. Next, use a spatula or palette knife to spread ganache evenly onto the first layer of cake. Try not to add too much, otherwise it will ooze out of the side of the cake (B).

A

B

3 Add the next layer of cake on top, then generously spread ganache onto the side and top of the cake with the spatula (**C–D**). It may be necessary to first add a thin layer of ganache over the whole cake to hold the crumbs of the cake in place ('crumb coating') and then add a second, thicker layer of ganache once the first layer is firm, to achieve an even covering.

4 Place the cake in the fridge until the ganache has set (usually about 1 hour).

Tip

To achieve a flawless covering, smooth the surface of a ganached cake with a hot knife or spatula, once the ganache has set.

Decorating cookies with royal icing

1 Using medium to stiff-peak pink royal icing in a piping bag fitted with a no. 2 round piping tip, pipe around the edge of 4 cookies (**A**).

2 Squeeze the thinned pink royal icing in the squeezy bottle into the outlined section of each cookie to 'flood' it with royal icing (B). Be careful not to overfill the cookie, otherwise the royal icing will leak over the edge of the outline. You may need to use a cocktail stick to drag royal icing towards the edges of the cookie (C).

3 Sometimes air bubbles may appear in the royal icing, so have a pin or cocktail stick on hand to pop them.

4 While the icing is still wet, squeeze small drops of the thinned white royal icing in the squeezy bottle onto the flooded surface of each cookie to create a polka dot pattern (D).

5 Repeat steps 1–4 on the remaining 3 cookies, using medium to stiff-peak white royal icing for the edging and thinned white royal icing for the flooding process, then thinned pink icing to add the polka dots.

6 Leave the cookies to dry for at least an hour, then pipe small dots around the edge of each cookie in either white or pink medium to stiff-peak royal icing (using a no. 2 round piping tube) to give them a professional finish (E).

7 Leave the cookies to dry for at least 4 hours before attaching them to the outside edge of the cake with ganache.

8 Tie the ribbon around the centre of the cookies to complete the cake.

Tip

Leave the cookies to dry under a lamp to achieve a shiny surface.

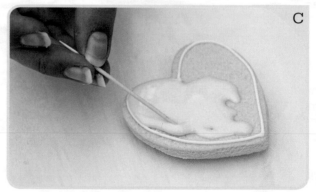

~ Baked with Love ~

Tip

Decorate some extra heart-shaped cookies to serve alongside your cake.

Focus on... HOW TO DECORATE COOKIES WITH ROYAL ICING

Go to

http://ideas.stitchcraftcreate.co.uk/ kitchen/videos/

for a video tutorial on how to flood a cookie with royal icing and add polka dots.

Baked with Love

39

Sew Pretty

This project focuses on a range of techniques that can be used to add texture to a cake. Although the cake has been designed for a baby shower, it could easily be adapted as a baby's birthday or christening cake and prepared in a range of colours.

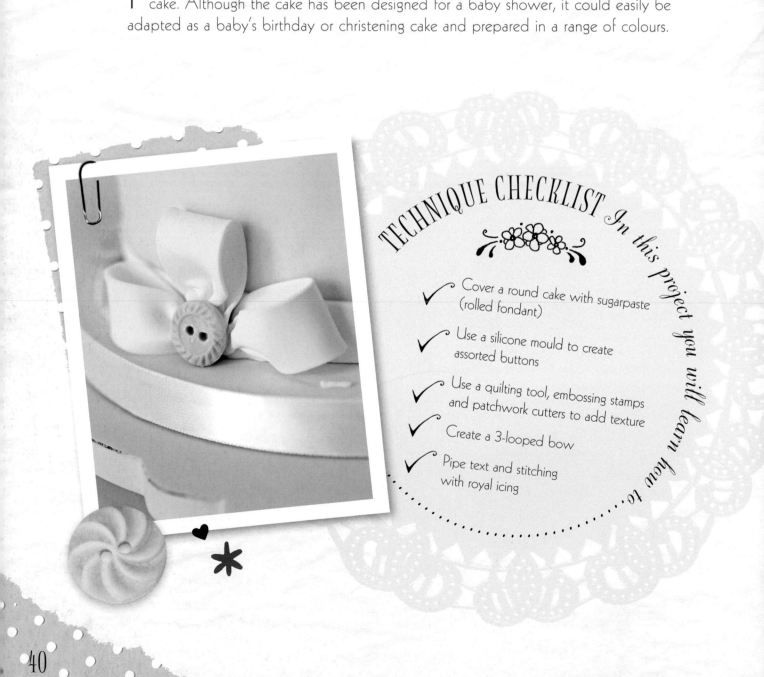

TECHNIQUE CHECKLIST In this project you will learn how to:

- ✓ Cover a round cake with sugarpaste (rolled fondant)

- ✓ Use a silicone mould to create assorted buttons

- ✓ Use a quilting tool, embossing stamps and patchwork cutters to add texture

- ✓ Create a 3-looped bow

- ✓ Pipe text and stitching with royal icing

YOU WILL NEED

- enough cake to cut out two 15cm (6in) rounds approx. 4cm (1½in) high

- 250g (9oz) buttercream

- 500g (1lb 2oz) shell pink sugarpaste (rolled fondant)

- 2 tbsp royal icing in a piping (pastry) bag fitted with a no. 1 round piping tube (tip)

- flower (petal/gum) paste: 30g (1oz) each dark pink, pale pink and white

- 15cm (6in) round cake card

- 20cm (8in) round cake board covered with shell pink sugarpaste and edged with ribbon

- button silicone mould (Alphabet Moulds patterned buttons AM0089)

- cutters: small squares 1.25cm (½in) and 0.95cm (⅜in) (Fine Cut); small heart plunger; garrett frill

- small patchwork cutters and embossing stamps (I used a small rose patchwork cutter and flower stamps from Holly Products)

- metal ruler

- pizza cutter (or ribbon cutting wheel)

- quilting tool

- cocktail stick (toothpick)

- Basic Cake Craft Kit (see Toolbox)

Preparing the cake

1 Trim the crust off the cake with a serrated knife. Place the round cake card on top of the cake and cut around the card, being careful to hold your knife straight and not at an angle (A). Repeat to cut out 2 rounds of cake. If the rounds are not even in height, gently pull a cake leveller through each one to make them uniform.

2 Use a spatula or palette knife to spread buttercream evenly on top of one layer of cake (B). Try not to add too much, otherwise it will ooze out of the side of the cake. Add the next layer of cake on top.

3 The next stage is to 'crumb coat' the cake to hold the crumbs of cake in place. Spread buttercream over the side and top of the cake with the spatula. It is easiest to add more buttercream than you need to start with and then scrape off any excess once it has been applied evenly to the whole cake (C). Aim to spread

A

B

the buttercream over the cake so that it is thin enough for the crumbs to show through.

4 Place the cake in the fridge until the crumb coat has set (about 1 hour). This will make the cake firm so that it is easier to apply the sugarpaste covering.

5 Once the crumb coat has set, knead the shell pink sugarpaste well until it is soft and pliable. Using a large non-stick rolling pin, roll out the sugarpaste in a rough circle shape on a non-stick board until it is approximately 5mm (³⁄₁₆in)

thick. Lift the sugarpaste off the board with the rolling pin and lay it gently over the cake (D).

6 Use your hands to smooth the sugarpaste over the top and down the side of the cake. Try to work as quickly as possible to make sure that the sugarpaste doesn't tear on the edge of the cake. As the sugarpaste is smoothed down the side, you may find that it starts to form pleats towards the base of the cake. If so, gently lift the paste away from the side of the cake and smooth it down so that it lays flat against the cake. Don't smooth over

the top of pleats, otherwise it will leave creases in your sugarpaste.

7 Trim off any excess sugarpaste from around the base of the cake with a small sharp knife.

8 Use a smoother — preferably 2 if you have them — to polish the top and side of the cake (E). This will help press out any air bubbles that may be trapped under the sugarpaste and will give your cake a nice smooth finish.

9 Attach the cake to the centre of the cake board with royal icing.

C
D
E

Buttons

1 Press a small ball of pink or white flower paste into the button silicone mould so that the flower paste is flush with the back of the mould (A). Use a small knife to trim off any excess paste if necessary.

2 Flex the mould to carefully remove the button and leave it to one side to dry (B). I have used 15 assorted buttons in my design, but feel free to add more or less to make your cake design unique.

3 Use royal icing to attach 5 buttons on top of the cake and 6 around the cake board (in

clusters of 2 buttons). Set aside 3 buttons to attach to the blanket and 1 button to add to the 3-looped bow.

A

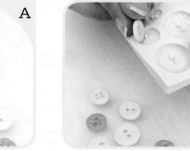
B

3-Looped bow

1 Roll out some white flower paste thinly into a strip at least 50cm (20in) long. Use a metal ruler and a pizza cutter (or ribbon cutting wheel) to cut the strip to 2cm (¾in) wide (**A**). Attach around the base of the cake with edible glue (**B**). Cut the strip to size with a knife — the ends should neatly touch each other.

2 Using a small knife or the pizza cutter, cut 3 strips of white flower paste 2cm (¾in) wide and 5cm (2in) long. Pleat both ends of each strip (**C**). Fold each strip in half and use edible glue to join the pleated sections of each strip together (**D**). This will create 3 separate loops.

3 Attach the loops over the join of the white strip with royal icing (**E**) — the pleated ends of each loop should touch each other. Disguise where the 3 loops join by adding a button to the centre with royal icing (**F**).

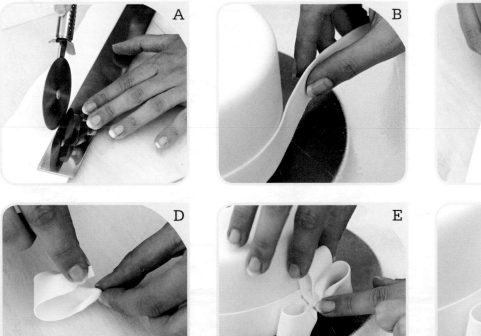

A

B

C

D

E

F

Stitches and writing

1 Using the no. 1 piping tube, pipe royal icing stitches around the cake on the cake board. It is always a good idea to practise piping on a board or plate before attempting to decorate the cake. Hold the piping bag in your right hand (if you are right-handed) and use your left hand to hold the bag steady. Don't start squeezing the icing out of the bag until the tube is in contact with the cake board surface. As the icing starts to come out of the tube, lift the tube from the surface. When the icing is the length you need, stop squeezing the bag and place the icing strand down on the surface. Try to pipe the lines at equal distances apart between the clusters of buttons on the cake board.

2 Use the same technique to pipe 'baby' or a name of your choice onto the top of the cake (A).

Tip

Freshly made royal icing is always preferable to use over old icing for piping, as it holds its shape and is stiffer and therefore easier to control.

Baby's patchwork blanket

1 Using a non-stick rolling pin, roll out some shell pink sugarpaste (approximately 100g/3½oz) into a rectangle about 3mm (⅛in) thick. Use a small knife to trim the sugarpaste so that it is about 12cm (4¾in) long and 9cm (3½in) wide (A).

2 Take one end of the rectangle in your hands and pleat it together (B). Leave the blanket under cling film (plastic wrap) until you are ready to decorate it, to prevent it from drying out.

3 Roll out some white, dark pink and pale pink flower paste finely with a small non-stick rolling pin on a non-stick board. Use the 1.25cm (½in) square cutter to cut out 12 squares (6 white and 6 pale pink) (C). Use the 0.95cm (⅜in) square cutter to cut out 3 dark pink squares.

4 Run the quilting tool around the edge of each white and pale pink square (D).

5 Press a small rose patchwork cutter into 2 pale pink squares and 1 white square (E).

6 Stick a small white button onto 2 white squares and 1 pale pink square with royal icing.

7 Use a small flower stamp to emboss the 3 dark pink squares (F). Attach the dark pink squares on top of 2 pale pink squares and 1 white square with edible glue.

8 Roll out some pink flower paste and use a plunger cutter to cut out 3 small hearts (G). Attach the hearts to the 3 remaining squares with edible glue.

9 Attach the 12 squares to the blanket with edible glue. The squares should be attached in alternating colours from the base (straight edge) of the blanket towards the pleated section in 3 rows of 4 squares (H).

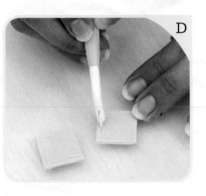

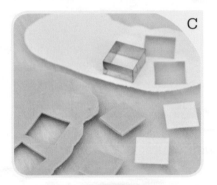

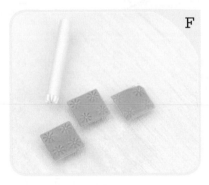

Tip

Experiment with patterns and make each square on the baby blanket different if desired.

~ Sew Pretty ~

10 Using a non-stick rolling pin, roll out some white flower paste thinly. Use a garrett frill cutter to cut out 3 rounds (**I**).

11 Use a small knife to make a cut in the rounds. Place the rounds on a non-stick board and gently rub a cocktail stick backwards and forwards over each scalloped edge to create a frilled effect (**J**).

12 Attach the frills to the underside of the blanket with edible glue, making sure they can be seen along the edge once the blanket is turned over (**K**). Add some frills to the top of the patchwork on the front of the blanket with edible glue if desired.

13 Attach the finished blanket to the top of the cake with royal icing.

Tip

Keep the garrett frill rounds under cling film (plastic wrap) until you are ready to frill them, to prevent them from drying out.

Focus on... HOW TO MOULD BUTTONS AND ADD PATTERNS TO SUGARPASTE

Go to

http://ideas.stitchcraftcreate.co.uk/kitchen/videos/

for a video tutorial on how to mould buttons and use a quilting tool and embossing stamps to add patterns to sugarpaste.

⌐ Sew Pretty ⌐

Frilly Fantasy in White

Simple yet elegant, this cake design is suitable for a formal occasion or a wedding. You'll be surprised just how easy it is to make (but don't tell your friends!) — the frilly flowers are quick to create and can be prepared ahead of time.

TECHNIQUE CHECKLIST
In this project you will learn how to:

✓ Stack, fill and 'crumb coat' a round cake with buttercream

✓ Cover a round cake with sugarpaste (rolled fondant)

✓ Add sugarpaste strips to a cake

✓ Use flower (gum/petal) paste to make delicate frilly flowers

YOU WILL NEED

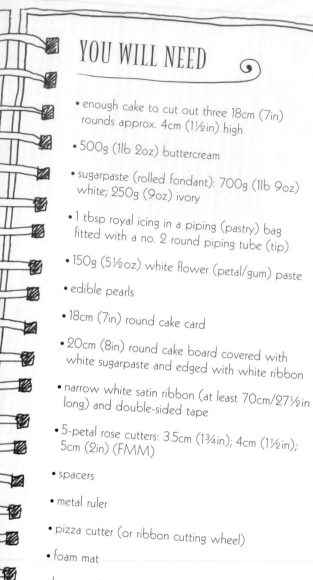

- enough cake to cut out three 18cm (7in) rounds approx. 4cm (1½in) high

- 500g (1lb 2oz) buttercream

- sugarpaste (rolled fondant): 700g (1lb 9oz) white; 250g (9oz) ivory

- 1 tbsp royal icing in a piping (pastry) bag fitted with a no. 2 round piping tube (tip)

- 150g (5½oz) white flower (petal/gum) paste

- edible pearls

- 18cm (7in) round cake card

- 20cm (8in) round cake board covered with white sugarpaste and edged with white ribbon

- narrow white satin ribbon (at least 70cm/27½in long) and double-sided tape

- 5-petal rose cutters: 3.5cm (1¾in); 4cm (1½in); 5cm (2in) (FMM)

- spacers

- metal ruler

- pizza cutter (or ribbon cutting wheel)

- foam mat

- bone tool

- paint palette

- tweezers

- Basic Cake Craft Kit (see Toolbox)

Preparing the cake

1 Trim the crust off the cake with a serrated knife (**A**). Place the round cake card on top of the cake and cut around the card, being careful to hold your knife straight and not at an angle (**B**). Repeat to cut out 3 rounds of cake. If the rounds are not even in height, gently pull a cake leveller through each one to make them uniform.

2 Use a spatula or palette knife to spread the buttercream evenly onto one layer of the cake (**C**). Try not to add too much, otherwise it will ooze out of the side of the cake.

3 Add the next layer of cake on top and spread with buttercream as before, then top with the final layer of cake.

A

B

4 The next stage is to 'crumb coat' the cake to hold the crumbs of cake in place. Spread buttercream over the side and top of the cake with the spatula. It is easiest to add more buttercream than you need to start with and then scrape off any excess once it has been applied evenly to the whole cake (**D**). Aim to spread the buttercream over the cake so that it is thin enough for the crumbs to show through.

5 Place the cake in the fridge until the crumb coat has set (usually about 1 hour). This will make the cake firm so that it is easier to apply the sugarpaste covering.

6 Once the crumb coat has set, knead the white sugarpaste well until it is soft and pliable. Using a large non-stick rolling pin, roll out the sugarpaste in a rough circle shape on a non-stick board until it is approximately 5mm (³⁄₁₆in) thick. Lift the sugarpaste off the board with the rolling pin and lay it gently over the cake (**E**).

7 Use your hands to smooth the paste over the top and down the side of the cake. Try to work as quickly as possible to make sure that the sugarpaste doesn't tear on the edge of the cake. As the sugarpaste is smoothed down the side, you may find that it starts to form pleats towards the base of the cake. If this happens, gently lift the sugarpaste away from the side of the cake and smooth it down so that it lays flat against the cake. Don't smooth over the top of pleats, otherwise it will leave creases in your sugarpaste.

8 Trim off any excess sugarpaste from around the base of the cake with a small sharp knife.

9 Use a smoother — preferably 2 if you have them — to polish the top and side of the cake (**F**). This will help press out any air bubbles that may be trapped under the sugarpaste and will give your cake a nice smooth finish.

10 Attach the cake to the centre of the cake board with royal icing.

Tip

After using the smoother to polish the cake, you may need to trim the sugarpaste around the base again with a knife to achieve a clean edge.

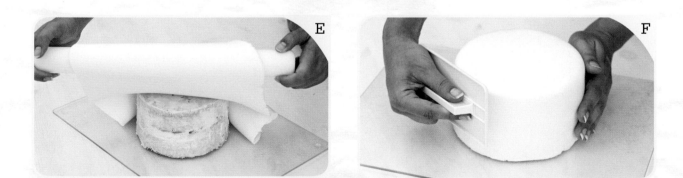

Frilly Fantasy in White

Ivory strips

1 Knead the ivory sugarpaste until it is soft and pliable. Using a non-stick rolling pin, roll out the sugarpaste on a non-stick board into a rectangle at least 13cm (5in) long in between 2 spacers. The spacers will ensure that the sugarpaste is rolled out to an even thickness (**A**).

2 Using a metal ruler and the pizza cutter (or ribbon cutting wheel), cut out 12 even strips 2cm (¾in) wide and 13cm (5in) long (**B**).

3 Attach each strip to the side of the cake with a little bit of water applied with a fine paintbrush (**C**). Each strip should start at the base of the cake and extend over the edge of the top of the cake by about 1cm (⅜in). If the strips are too long, use a small knife to cut them to size (**D**). You can use the ruler to ensure that the strips are evenly spaced around the side of the cake – I placed mine 2.5cm (1in) apart.

4 Once all the strips have been attached, trim the base of the cake with the ribbon, using double-sided tape to secure it in place.

Tip

Keep any leftover sugarpaste, as well as any remaining flower paste used for making the flowers, wrapped tightly in cling film (plastic wrap) at room temperature so that it doesn't dry out and you can use it again.

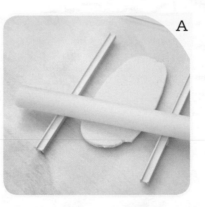
A

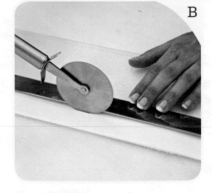
B

C

D

Frilly flowers

1 Knead the white flower paste until it is soft and pliable. You will know when it is ready to use because it will be stretchy like chewing gum.

2 Using a small non-stick rolling pin, roll out the white flower paste thinly on a non-stick board. Use the 5-petal rose cutters to cut out 12 small, 12 medium and 12 large flowers and place them on a foam mat (A).

3 Use a bone tool to gently thin and ruffle the edges of each petal of the flowers (B).

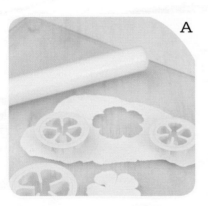

A

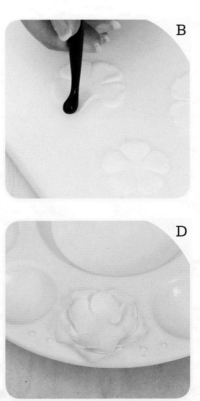

B

Tip

Keep the flowers under cling film (plastic wrap) until you are ready to ruffle the edges, to prevent them from drying out.

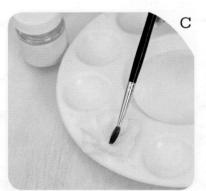

C

D

4 To make one frilly flower, gently place the largest flower into a well of a paint palette. Arrange the petals so that they overlap and are in the position in which you would like them to dry. Using a fine paintbrush, add a little bit of edible glue to the centre of the large petal (C) and place the medium-sized flower on top of it, again arranging the petals so that they overlap (D).

Frilly Fantasy in White

5 Add more edible glue to the centre of the medium flower and place the smallest flower on top. You may need to use a tool, such as a ball or bone tool, or the end of a paintbrush to push the last layer of the flower into position (**E**). Repeat this process to make 12 flowers.

6 Pipe a small amount of royal icing into the centre of each flower (**F**) and then, using tweezers, arrange edible pearls in each flower centre (**G**).

7 Allow the flowers to dry overnight, then attach them to the top of the cake, in line with each ivory strip, with a small amount of royal icing.

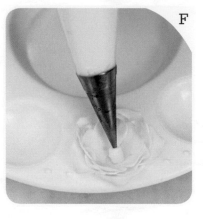

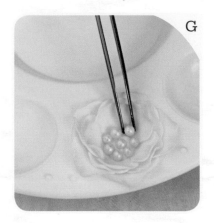

Tip

You can add more layers to your flowers to make them even frillier, but remember to add them in decreasing size with the largest flowers on the bottom of the paint palette and the smallest flowers on top.

Tip

If you want each layer of the flower to be quite separate, use small pieces of kitchen paper (paper towel) or a napkin to separate the layers while they are drying. Remember to remove the paper before attaching the flowers to the cake.

Tip

Make extra flowers as decorations for cupcakes to complement the cake.

Focus on ... HOW TO MAKE A FRILLY FLOWER

Go to

**http://ideas.stitchcraftcreate.co.uk/
kitchen/videos/**

for a video tutorial on how to make white
frilly flowers from flower paste.

Frilly Fantasy in White

Pinwheel Fun

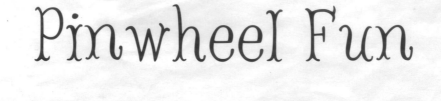

This delightful celebration cake is decorated with pinwheels made using edible icing sheets and flower paste. You can use pre-printed icing sheets, or choose any pattern you like and have it printed onto an icing sheet with edible ink cartridges. If you have time, make some extra pinwheels to add on top of cookies or cupcakes to complement the cake centrepiece.

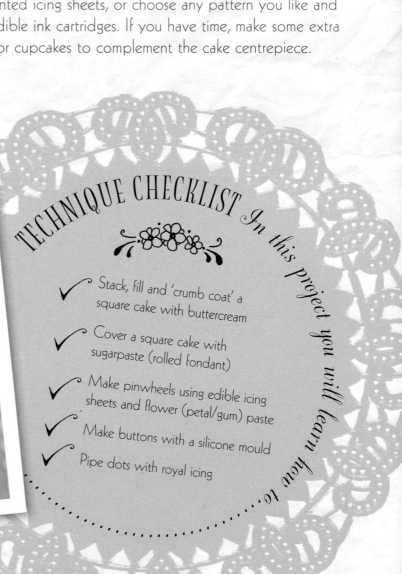

TECHNIQUE CHECKLIST In this project you will learn how to...

✓ Stack, fill and 'crumb coat' a square cake with buttercream

✓ Cover a square cake with sugarpaste (rolled fondant)

✓ Make pinwheels using edible icing sheets and flower (petal/gum) paste

✓ Make buttons with a silicone mould

✓ Pipe dots with royal icing

YOU WILL NEED

- enough cake to cut out three 15cm (6in) squares approx. 5cm (2in) high

- 600g (1lb 5oz) buttercream

- 1kg (2lb 4oz) pale yellow sugarpaste (rolled fondant)

- 5 tbsp royal icing in piping (pastry) bag fitted with a no. 2 round piping tube (tip)

- 1 edible icing sheet printed with a design of your choice (I used a pink polka dot sheet from Culpitt)

- flower (petal/gum) paste: 30g (1oz) each pale blue, pale green and blue; 20g (¾oz) white

- 15cm (6in) square cake card

- 20cm (8in) square cake board covered with pale yellow sugarpaste and edged with ribbon

- ribbon (at least 70cm/27½in long) and double-sided tape

- metal square cutters: 5cm (2in); 4.5cm (1¾in)

- button silicone mould

- white paper-covered florist wire (at least 26-gauge)

- posy pick

- scissors

- Basic Cake Craft Kit (see Toolbox)

Preparing the cake

1 Trim the crust off the cake with a serrated knife. Place the square cake card on top of the cake and cut around the card, being careful to hold your knife straight and not at an angle (**A**). Repeat to cut out 3 squares of cake. If the squares are not even in height, gently pull a cake leveller through each one to make them uniform (**B**).

2 Use a spatula or palette knife to spread the buttercream evenly onto the first layer of cake. Try not to add too much, otherwise it will ooze out of the side of the cake. Add the next layer of cake on top and spread with buttercream as before (**C**), then top with the final layer of cake.

A

B

3 The next stage is to 'crumb coat' the cake to hold the crumbs of cake in place. Spread buttercream over the sides and top of the cake with the spatula (D). It is easiest to add more buttercream than you need to start with and then scrape off any excess once it has been applied evenly to the whole cake. Aim to spread the buttercream over the cake so that it is thin enough for the crumbs to show through.

4 Place the cake in the fridge until the crumb coat has set (usually about 1 hour). This will make the cake firm so that it is easier to apply the sugarpaste covering.

5 Once the crumb coat has set, knead the pale yellow sugarpaste well until it is soft and pliable. Using a large non-stick rolling pin, roll out the sugarpaste in a rough square shape on a non-stick board until it is

approximately 5mm (³⁄₁₆in) thick. Lift the sugarpaste off the board with the rolling pin and lay it gently over the cake (E).

6 Use your hands to smooth the sugarpaste over the top and down the corners of the cake. Try to work as quickly as possible to make sure that the sugarpaste doesn't tear on the edges or corners of the cake.

7 Next, use your hands to smooth the sugarpaste over the sides of the cake. As the sugarpaste is smoothed down the sides, you may find that it starts to form pleats towards the base of the cake. If so, gently lift the sugarpaste away from the side of the cake and smooth it down so that it lays flat against the cake (F). Don't smooth over the top of pleats, otherwise it will leave creases in your sugarpaste.

❧ Pinwheel Fun ❧

8 Trim off any excess sugarpaste from around the base of the cake with a small sharp knife.

9 Use a smoother — preferably 2 if you have them — to polish the top and sides of the cake. This will help press out any air bubbles that may be trapped under the sugarpaste and will give your cake a nice smooth finish.

10 Attach the cake to the centre of the cake board with royal icing.

11 Trim the base of the cake with ribbon, making sure that it is flush with the cake board, and secure it in place with double-sided tape.

12 Place the cake onto a turntable, if you have one, to make it easier to turn the cake as you are piping. Pipe evenly spaced dots of royal icing onto each side and the top of the cake (**G**). You can pipe as many dots as you like.

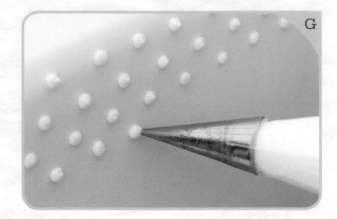

Tip

If your piped dots have pointy peaks, you can use a damp paintbrush to push them into a rounded shape.

Pinwheels

1 Use the 5cm (2in) square cutter to cut out 6 squares and the 4.5cm (1¾in) square cutter to cut out 3 squares from the edible icing sheet (**A**) — the sheet is often quite rigid, so you will have to press firmly to ensure a clean cut.

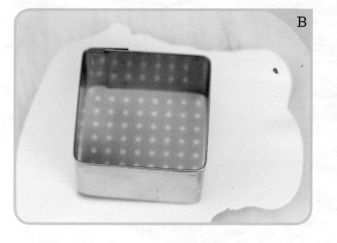

2 Turn the squares pattern-side down onto a board and add a little bit of cooled boiled water to the back of them with a fine paintbrush.

3 Using a non-stick rolling pin, roll out the 3 different-coloured flower pastes thinly on a non-stick board and then place the edible icing squares, pattern-side up, on top of the flower paste. Rub your fingers gently over the squares to ensure that they stick firmly to the flower paste underneath. Use the square metal cutters to cut out the flower paste so that it is the same size as the edible icing squares (**B**).

4 Using scissors, cut diagonally from each corner of the square to 1cm (½in) from the centre, to create 4 segments (**C**).

5 Place the square pattern-side down onto a board. Starting at the top right-hand corner, work clockwise around the square folding one corner of each segment towards the centre (**D–E**). If the flower paste is a bit dry, you can use some edible glue to hold the sections of the pinwheel in place.

Tip

I have used three different colours of flower paste for the pinwheels, but you can use as many or as few as you wish.

~ Pinwheel Fun ~

6 To create little buttons for the centre of each pinwheel, press a small ball of white flower paste into a button silicone mould (F), then flex the mould to remove the button (G).

7 Attach the buttons to the centre of each pinwheel using royal icing (H).

Decorating the cake

1 Use royal icing to attach 2 large and 1 small pinwheel up the front face of the cake. Attach a large pinwheel to the centre of the 3 remaining sides of the cake.

2 Insert the florist wire into the base of the remaining pinwheels. If the wire is quite thin, you may need to double it over so that it is strong enough to support the weight of the pinwheel (A).

3 Insert the wired pinwheels into a posy pick and press them into the centre of the top of the cake.

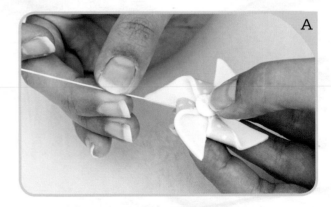

WARNING!
Any pinwheels that contain wire should not be eaten.

Tip

Make some extra pinwheels and attach them to cookies or cupcakes with royal icing to complement the cake.

Focus on... HOW TO MAKE ICING PINWHEELS

Go to
**http://ideas.stitchcraftcreate.co.uk/
kitchen/videos/**
for a video tutorial on how to make pinwheels using printed edible icing sheets.

Pinwheel Fun

Doily Delight

Doilies have become increasingly popular for displaying and ornamenting cakes, and this project demonstrates how to make edible ones from flower paste. Also included are instructions for creating an assortment of pastel blossoms, making this cake perfect for a springtime tea party.

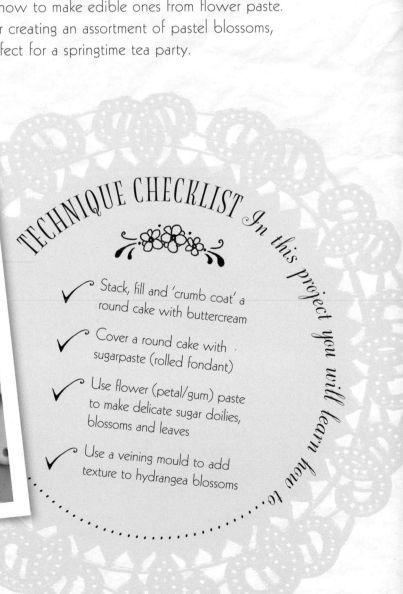

TECHNIQUE CHECKLIST In this project you will learn how to:

✓ Stack, fill and 'crumb coat' a round cake with buttercream

✓ Cover a round cake with sugarpaste (rolled fondant)

✓ Use flower (petal/gum) paste to make delicate sugar doilies, blossoms and leaves

✓ Use a veining mould to add texture to hydrangea blossoms

YOU WILL NEED

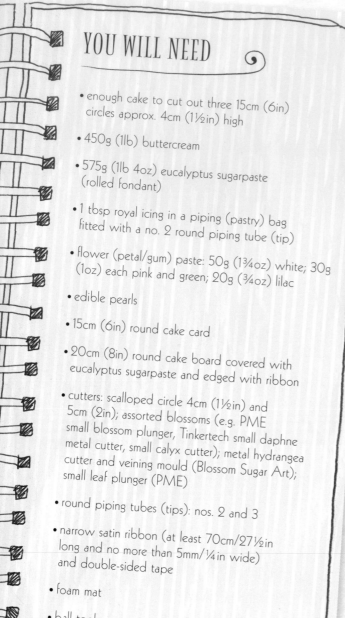

- enough cake to cut out three 15cm (6in) circles approx. 4cm (1½in) high

- 450g (1lb) buttercream

- 575g (1lb 4oz) eucalyptus sugarpaste (rolled fondant)

- 1 tbsp royal icing in a piping (pastry) bag fitted with a no. 2 round piping tube (tip)

- flower (petal/gum) paste: 50g (1¾oz) white; 30g (1oz) each pink and green; 20g (¾oz) lilac

- edible pearls

- 15cm (6in) round cake card

- 20cm (8in) round cake board covered with eucalyptus sugarpaste and edged with ribbon

- cutters: scalloped circle 4cm (1½in) and 5cm (2in); assorted blossoms (e.g. PME small blossom plunger, Tinkertech small daphne metal cutter, small calyx cutter); metal hydrangea cutter and veining mould (Blossom Sugar Art); small leaf plunger (PME)

- round piping tubes (tips): nos. 2 and 3

- narrow satin ribbon (at least 70cm/27½in long and no more than 5mm/¼in wide) and double-sided tape

- foam mat

- ball tool

- Basic Cake Craft Kit (see Toolbox)

Preparing the cake

1 Trim the crust off the cake with a serrated knife. Place the round cake card on top of the cake and cut around the card, being careful to hold your knife straight and not at an angle (A). Repeat to cut out 3 rounds of cake. If the rounds are not even in height, gently pull a cake leveller through each one to make them uniform.

2 Use a spatula or palette knife to spread buttercream evenly onto the cake (B). Try not to add too much, otherwise it will ooze out of the side of the cake. Add the next layer of cake on top and spread with buttercream as before, then top with the final layer of cake.

A

B

3 The next stage is to 'crumb coat' the cake to hold the crumbs of cake in place. Spread buttercream over the side and top of the cake with the spatula. It is easiest to add more buttercream than you need to start with and then scrape off any excess once it has been applied evenly to the whole cake (C). Aim to spread the buttercream over the cake so that it is thin enough for the crumbs to show through.

4 Place the cake in the fridge until the crumb coat has set (usually about 1 hour). This will make the cake firm so that it is easier to apply the sugarpaste covering.

5 Once the crumb coat has set, knead the eucalyptus sugarpaste well until it is soft and pliable. Using a large non-stick rolling pin, roll out the sugarpaste in a rough circle shape on a non-stick board until it is approximately 5mm (³⁄₁₆in) thick. Lift the sugarpaste off the board with the rolling pin and lay it gently over the cake (D).

6 Use your hands to smooth the paste over the top and down the side of the cake (E). Try to work as quickly as possible to make sure that the sugarpaste doesn't tear on the edge of the cake. As the sugarpaste is smoothed down the side, you may find that it starts to form pleats towards the base of the cake. If this happens, gently lift the sugarpaste away from the side of the cake and smooth it down so that it lays flat against the cake. Don't smooth over the top of pleats, otherwise it will leave a crease in your sugarpaste.

7 Trim off any excess sugarpaste from around the base of the cake with a small sharp knife.

8 Use a smoother – preferably 2 if you have them – to polish the top and side of the cake. This will help press out any air bubbles that may be trapped under the sugarpaste and will give your cake a nice smooth finish.

9 Attach the cake to the centre of the cake board with royal icing.

Sugar doilies

1 Knead the white flower paste until it is soft and pliable. You will know when it is ready to use because it will be stretchy like chewing gum.

2 Using a small non-stick rolling pin, roll out the white flower paste thinly onto a non-stick board and use the 4cm (1½in) scalloped circle cutter to cut out 2 scalloped circles and the 5cm (2in) cutter to cut out 7 scalloped circles (**A**).

3 Use the end of the nos. 2 and 3 piping tubes to cut out small holes in the scalloped circles to create a doily pattern. You can make the design as simple or as detailed as you desire, but I have used the no. 3 tube to cut out a hole in each scalloped section and then the no. 2 tube to cut out 2 smaller holes between each scalloped section (**B**).

4 Once you have created your doily pattern, cut 5 of the larger doilies in half and stick them around the base of the cake with a little water or edible glue applied to the back of them with a fine paintbrush. The flat edge should touch the cake board (**C**).

5 Trim the base of the cake with the satin ribbon, securing it in place with double-sided tape.

6 Attach the remaining 2 large and 2 small doilies up the front of the cake, overlapping them slightly and securing them in place with a little water or edible glue.

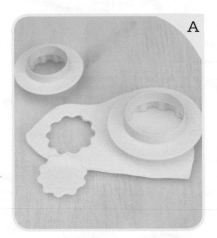

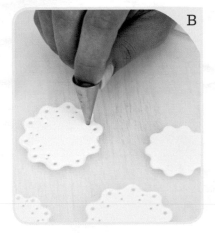

Tip
Create fancier doilies by using small cutters, such as teardrop shapes, to cut out other patterns.

Doily Delight

Assorted blossoms

1 Knead the white and pink flower pastes separately until soft and pliable.

2 Using a small non-stick rolling pin, roll out the flower paste thinly on a non-stick board and cut out an assortment of daphnes, blossoms and star flowers (using a calyx cutter), then place them on a foam mat (A). You can make as many flowers as you like for your cake, but I cut out 9 daphnes (5 white and 4 pink), 2 star flowers in pink and 7 small blossoms in pink. Wrap up the leftover paste in cling film (plastic wrap) to use later.

3 Press the small end of a ball tool into the centre of each flower to shape it (B). The more you press down, the more your flowers will form into a cupped shape. If your ball tool sticks to the flower as you press into it (this often occurs when the flower paste is very fresh and sticky), leave the flowers to dry for a few minutes before shaping them. But don't leave them for too long, otherwise they will crack when you press the ball tool into them.

4 Pipe a small dot of royal icing into the centre of each flower, and then leave them to dry for about an hour. If you prefer, you can attach edible pearls to the centre of the flowers using royal icing.

Ruffled blossoms

1 Using a small non-stick rolling pin, roll out the white flower paste thinly on a non-stick board. Cut out 3 scalloped circles with the 4cm (1½in) scalloped cutter.

2 Fold each circle in half and then in half again. Squeeze the base of each blossom together to secure the ruffles in place.

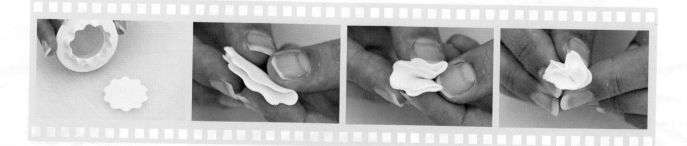

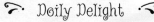

Hydrangeas

1 Using a small non-stick rolling pin, roll out the lilac flower paste thinly on a non-stick board. Use the metal hydrangea cutter to cut out however many hydrangeas you want to use (**A**) – I have used 3 in my design.

2 Place the hydrangea flowers one at a time into one side of the veining mould (**B**). Close the mould over the top of the flower and press firmly to imprint the hydrangea pattern into both sides of the flower.

3 Open the veining mould, then remove the flower and leave to one side to dry.

Tip

If the flower paste sticks to the veining mould, grease the mould with a little white vegetable fat (shortening) before imprinting each flower.

A

B

Tip

The hydrangeas can be shaped into a more cupped shape by pressing a ball tool into their centres (before they have dried) while they are on a foam mat.

Leaves

1 Knead the green flower paste until soft and pliable. Using a small non-stick rolling pin, roll out the flower paste thinly on a non-stick board. Press a small leaf plunger cutter firmly into the paste, and then push down the plunger to imprint veins into the leaf (**A**).

2 Pinch the base of each leaf into a 'V' shape (**B**), then leave to one side to dry. You can make as many leaves as you like for your cake, but I have used 5 in my design.

Decorating the cake

1 When you are ready to decorate the cake, pipe a small amount of royal icing onto the back of each flower and leaf and stick them into position on the cake and cake board.

2 To complete the design, use royal icing to attach a few edible pearls to the cake.

Focus on... HOW TO MAKE SUGAR DOILIES AND ASSORTED BLOSSOMS AND LEAVES

Go to
http://ideas.stitchcraftcreate.co.uk/ kitchen/videos/
for a video tutorial on how to make doilies, blossoms and leaves using flower paste.

⌁ Doily Delight ⌁

Brush Embroidery Bliss

This enchanting cake uses a technique called brush embroidery to create a delicate lace effect. Brush embroidery involves using a damp paintbrush to smudge lines of either royal icing or buttercream to achieve a feathered effect. The technique itself is quite easy to master, but it is time consuming. If time is limited, you can modify the design to feature fewer tea roses.

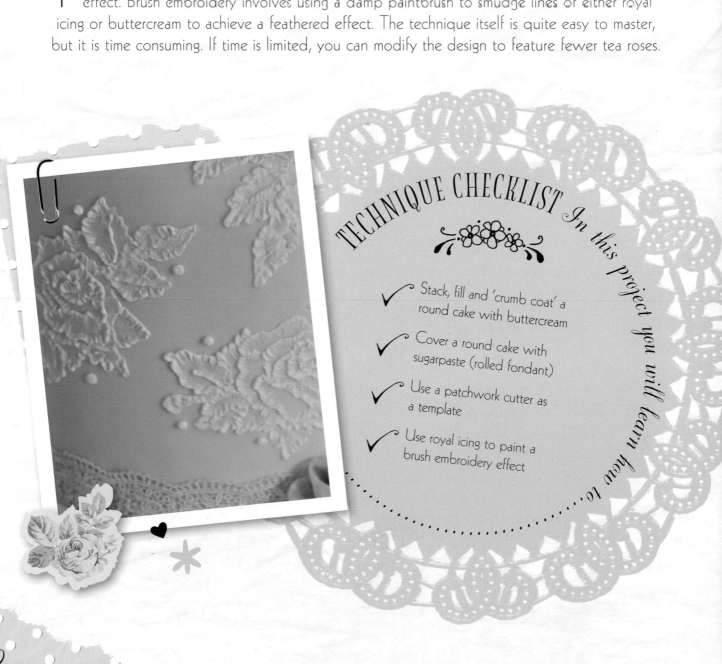

TECHNIQUE CHECKLIST In this project you will learn how to…

✓ Stack, fill and 'crumb coat' a round cake with buttercream

✓ Cover a round cake with sugarpaste (rolled fondant)

✓ Use a patchwork cutter as a template

✓ Use royal icing to paint a brush embroidery effect

- enough cake to cut out four 20cm (8in) rounds approx. 4cm (1½in) high

- 800g (1lb 12oz) buttercream

- 1.4kg (3lb 1oz) duck egg sugarpaste (rolled fondant)

- 7 tbsp royal icing in a piping (pastry) bag fitted with a no. 2 round piping tube (tip)

- 20cm (8in) round cake card

- 20cm (8in) round cake board

- ribbon or lace (at least 70cm/27½in long and 3cm/1¼in wide) and double-sided tape

- rose patchwork cutter (Tea Rose PC017)

- fine paintbrush

- Basic Cake Craft Kit (see Toolbox)

Preparing the cake

1 Trim the crust off the cake with a serrated knife. Place the round cake card on top of the cake and cut around the card, being careful to hold your knife straight and not at an angle (**A**). Repeat this step to cut out 4 rounds of cake. If the rounds are not even in height, gently pull a cake leveller through each one to make them uniform.

2 Use a spatula or palette knife to spread the buttercream evenly onto the first layer of cake (**B**). Try not to add too much, otherwise it will ooze out of the side of the cake. Add the next 2 layers of cake on top, spreading buttercream in between them as before, then top with the final layer of cake.

Tip

Place the cake on a turntable, if you have one, when 'crumb coating' to make it easier to turn the cake as you are applying the buttercream.

A

B

3 The next stage is to 'crumb coat' the cake to hold the crumbs of cake in place. Spread buttercream over the side and top of the cake with the spatula. It is easiest to add more buttercream than you need to start with and then scrape off any excess once it has been applied evenly to the whole cake (C). Aim to spread the buttercream over the cake so that it is thin enough for the crumbs to show through.

4 Place the cake in the fridge until the crumb coat has set (usually about 1 hour). This will make the cake firm so that it is easier to apply the sugarpaste covering.

5 Once the crumb coat has set, knead the duck egg sugarpaste well until it is soft and pliable. Using a large non-stick rolling pin, roll out the sugarpaste in a rough circle shape on a non-stick board until it is approximately 5mm (³⁄₁₆in) thick. Lift the sugarpaste off the board with the rolling pin and lay it gently over the cake (D).

6 Use your hands to smooth the paste over the top and down the side of the cake. Try to work as quickly as possible to make sure that the sugarpaste doesn't tear on the edge of the cake. As the sugarpaste is smoothed down the side, you may find that it starts to form pleats towards the base of the cake. If so, gently lift the sugarpaste away from the side of the cake and smooth it down so that it lays flat against the cake (E). Don't smooth over the top of pleats, otherwise it will leave creases in your sugarpaste.

7 Trim off any excess sugarpaste from around the base of the cake with a small sharp knife.

8 Use a smoother – preferably 2 if you have them – to polish the top and side of the cake. This will help press out any air bubbles that may be trapped under the sugarpaste and will give your cake a nice smooth finish.

Brush Embroidery Bliss

9 Attach the cake to the cake board with some royal icing.

10 Trim the cake and cake board with ribbon, securing it in place with double-sided tape. The ribbon should cover the join between the cake board and the cake.

Tip

You could add a (non-edible) brooch to the base of the cake for extra decorative detail.

Brush embroidery

1 Press the rose patchwork cutter into the side and top of the cake where you intend to add the brush embroidery effect. You will need to do this before the sugarpaste has dried, otherwise the paste will crack. After removing the patchwork cutter you will see an embossed pattern of the tea rose, which will act as the template for your brush embroidery design (A).

2 Pipe royal icing around the outside edge of the tea rose (B). You may wish to pipe only a small section at first, to prevent the royal icing from drying out before you have time to paint it.

3 Use a damp fine paintbrush to drag the royal icing towards the centre of the tea rose (C). It is best to work in quick, short strokes to achieve a feathered effect. Clean the paintbrush with water frequently to create distinct lines of royal icing. Be careful to dab the paintbrush on kitchen paper (paper towel) after it has been cleaned in water to make sure that it is not too wet before applying it to the royal icing.

4 Repeat the technique for the inner sections of the tea rose until the design is complete.

5 Pipe some royal icing dots around the tea roses if desired to complete the design.

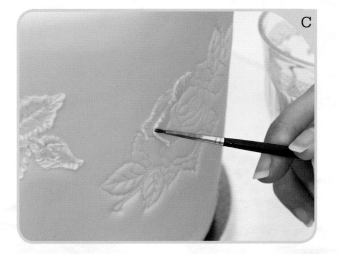

C

Tip

Place the cake on a turntable if you have one. This will allow you to turn the cake without accidentally smudging some of the royal icing patterns before they have dried.

Focus on... HOW TO CREATE A BRUSH EMBROIDERY DESIGN WITH ROYAL ICING

Go to
http://ideas.stitchcraftcreate.co.uk/ kitchen/videos/
for a video tutorial on how to add a brush embroidery design to a cake with royal icing.

↶ Brush Embroidery Bliss ↷

Strawberry Tea Cake

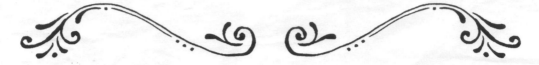

A few steps beyond the standard technique for covering a round cake results in this impressive novelty cake, realistically styled to mimic an iced and fresh strawberry-decorated gateau. The missing slice reveals a faux filling of jam and cream, but you can easily adapt the design to use a different colour scheme and filling, such as yellow or brown sugarpaste strips to resemble lemon curd or chocolate.

TECHNIQUE CHECKLIST *In this project you will learn how to...*

✓ Stack, fill and 'crumb coat' a cake that is missing a slice with buttercream

✓ Cover a cake that is missing a slice with sugarpaste (rolled fondant)

✓ Use sugarpaste to make strawberries and blossoms

YOU WILL NEED

- enough cake to cut out three 15cm (6in) circles approx. 4cm (1½in) high

- 400g (14oz) buttercream

- sugarpaste (rolled fondant): 100g (3½oz) each peach and red; 500g (1lb 2oz) shell pink; 200g (7oz) white; 30g (1oz) each dark pink and green

- 1 tbsp royal icing in a piping (pastry) bag fitted with a no. 2 round piping tube (tip)

- 15cm (6in) round cake card

- 20cm (8in) round cake board covered with shell pink sugarpaste and edged with ribbon

- cutters: small calyx; small blossom plunger (PME)

- long, thin paintbrush (or dowel)

- scribing tool

- foam mat

- ball tool

- Basic Cake Craft Kit (see Toolbox)

Preparing the cake

1 Trim the crust off the cake with a serrated knife. Place the round cake card on top of the cake and cut around the card, being careful to hold your knife straight and not at an angle (A). Repeat this step to cut out 3 rounds of cake. If the rounds are not even in height, gently pull a cake leveller through each one to make them uniform.

2 Use a spatula or palette knife to spread the buttercream evenly onto the first layer of cake. Try not to add too much, otherwise it will ooze out of the side of the cake. Add the next layer of cake on top and spread the buttercream as before (B), then top with the final layer of cake.

A

B

Tip

Add chopped fresh strawberries to the buttercream filling for an extra decadent treat.

⌁ Strawberry Tea Cake ⌁

3 Using a sharp knife, cut out a large slice of cake (C).

4 The next stage is to 'crumb coat' the cake to hold the crumbs of cake in place. Spread buttercream over the side and top of the cake with the spatula. It is easiest to add more buttercream than you need to start with and then scrape off any excess once it has been applied evenly to the whole cake. Remember also to add buttercream into the section where the slice was removed (D). Aim to spread the buttercream over the cake so that it is thin enough for the crumbs to show through.

5 Place the cake in the fridge until the crumb coat has set (about 1 hour). This will make the cake firm so that it is easier to apply the sugarpaste covering.

6 Once the crumb coat has set, knead the peach sugarpaste well until it is soft and pliable. Using a non-stick rolling pin, roll out the sugarpaste into a strip at least 11.5cm (4½in) high and long enough to cover where the slice of cake has been removed. Using the end of a long paintbrush (or a dowel), press the strip of sugarpaste into the cut-out section and use your hands to smooth it against the cake (E). Trim the edges of the paste with a knife in line with the base and top of the cake.

7 Using a large non-stick rolling pin, roll out the shell pink sugarpaste in a rough circle shape on a non-stick board until it is 5mm (³⁄₁₆in) thick. Lift the paste off the board with the rolling pin and lay it gently over the cake (F).

Tip

If the buttercream doesn't spread easily while 'crumb coating', add a little water to the buttercream to achieve a smooth consistency. This will prevent the cake from tearing as you spread on the buttercream.

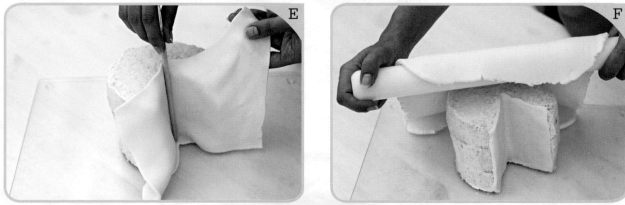

Strawberry Tea Cake

8 Use your hands to smooth the paste over the top and down the side of the cake, but not into the cut-out section. Try to work as quickly as possible to make sure that the paste doesn't tear on the edges of the cake. As the sugarpaste is smoothed down the side, you may find that it starts to form pleats towards the base of the cake. If so, gently lift the sugarpaste away from the side of the cake and smooth it down so that it lays flat against the cake. Don't smooth over the top of pleats, otherwise it will leave creases in your sugarpaste. Trim the paste around the cut-out section (G) and then use a finger to gently blend the peach and shell pink sugarpastes together where they meet.

9 Trim off any excess sugarpaste from around the base of the cake with a small sharp knife.

Tip

Although not shown in this project, you can also cover the slice of cake with sugarpaste and display it alongside your main cake.

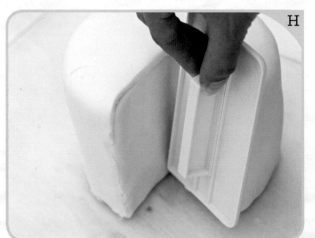

10 Use a smoother to polish the top and sides of the cake and inside the cut-out section. This will help press out any air bubbles that might be trapped under the sugarpaste and will give your cake a nice smooth finish (H).

Strawberry Tea Cake

11 Roll out the white sugarpaste into a rough circle at least 20cm (8in) in diameter. Place the round cake card on the centre of the sugarpaste. This will act as a template for the top of your cake. Use a knife to cut out a wavy edge about 2cm (¾in) away from the cake card (**I**). Gently place the white sugarpaste on top of the cake and smooth the wavy edges over the side of the cake (**J**). Use a knife to trim the sugarpaste that hangs into the cut-out section so that it is flush with the top of the cake (**K**).

12 To decorate the cut-out section, roll out 2 thin strips of white sugarpaste and 2 thin strips of dark pink sugarpaste (slightly thinner than the white strips). Attach the pink strips to the centre of each white strip using edible glue (**L**). These strips will represent the cake filling. If you would prefer a different faux filling, replace the pink strip with another coloured paste, e.g. brown to represent chocolate or yellow for lemon curd.

13 Attach the strips horizontally across the cut-out section of the cake with edible glue. It is easiest to use the end of a long, thin paintbrush to guide the strips into the narrowest point (**M**). Trim off any excess paste with a knife.

14 Attach the cake to the centre of the cake board with royal icing.

Tip

The strips representing the cake filling don't need to be perfectly straight if you want the filling to look like it's oozing out of the cake.

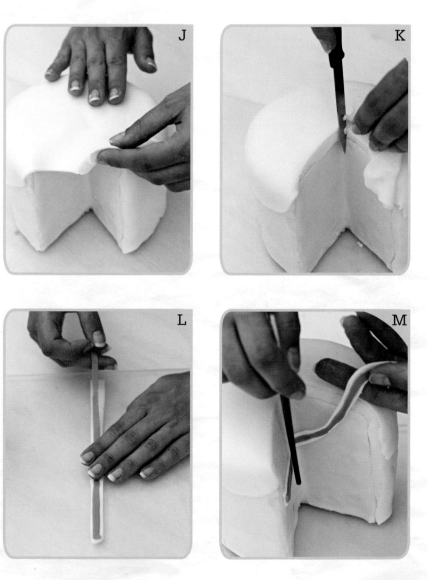

⌒ Strawberry Tea Cake ⌒

Strawberries

1 Roll out a ball of red sugarpaste into a strawberry shape approximately 5cm (2in) long. Repeat this process to make 6 strawberries (A).

2 Roll out the green sugarpaste and use the small calyx cutter to cut out 6 calyxes (A). Attach a calyx to the top of each strawberry with edible glue.

3 Roll 6 small stems of green sugarpaste and attach one to each calyx with edible glue (B).

4 Use a scribing tool to indent little holes all over the surface of each strawberry to resemble seeds (C).

A

B

Tip

Make the strawberries in advance and keep them in a container at room temperature away from moisture.

C

Strawberry Tea Cake

Blossoms

1 To make the blossoms, roll out some pink sugarpaste thinly and use the small blossom plunger cutter to cut out 6 blossoms (A). Place the blossoms on a foam mat and use a ball tool to shape them (B).

2 Add a dot of royal icing to the centre of each blossom and leave them to dry.

3 Attach the blossoms to the strawberries with edible glue.

4 Attach the strawberry decorations to the top of the cake with royal icing.

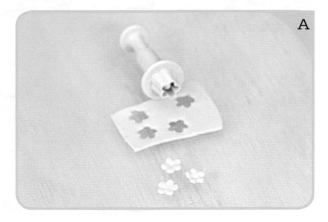

A

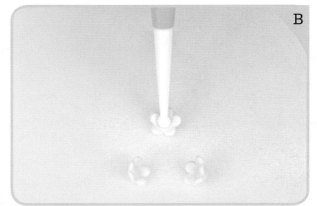

B

Tip

Make extra blossoms to add to the cake board in clusters for a more elaborate cake design.

Focus on... MAKING SUGAR STRAWBERRIES AND BLOSSOMS

Go to
http://ideas.stitchcraftcreate.co.uk/ kitchen/videos/
for a video tutorial on how to make strawberries and blossoms with sugarpaste.

Strawberry Tea Cake

A Rose & Lace Romance

Decorated with pretty handmade roses, this elegant cake also features a delicate lace pattern created by applying royal icing to a stencil. The techniques in this project are not as tricky as they may appear and can be used for other bakes such as cupcakes and cookies.

TECHNIQUE CHECKLIST *In this project you will learn how to:*

✓ Stack, fill and 'crumb coat' a square cake with buttercream

✓ Cover a square cake with sugarpaste (rolled fondant)

✓ Make small and large roses with leaves from flower (petal/gum) paste

✓ Use royal icing and a stencil to create a pretty lace pattern

YOU WILL NEED

- enough cake to cut out three 15cm (6in) squares approx. 5cm (2in) high

- 600g (1lb 5oz) buttercream

- 1kg (2lb 4oz) pale green sugarpaste (rolled fondant)

- 7 tbsp royal icing for stencilled lace pattern; plus 2 tbsp in piping (pastry) bag fitted with a no. 2 round piping tube (tip) for attaching roses and leaves

- flower (petal/gum) paste: 100g (3½oz) pale pink; 20g (¾oz) green

- edible pearl lustre dust (I used Starlight Comet White edible rainbow dust)

- 20cm (8in) square cake board covered with pale green sugarpaste and edged with ribbon

- 15cm (6in) square cake card

- Designer Stencils Lace Set #1 (C362)

- cutters: 9cm (3½in) 5-petal rose; 4cm (1½in) 5-petal rose; large and small leaf (I used 2.7cm/1in and 2cm/¾in)

- ribbon (at least 70cm/27½in long) and double-sided tape

- thick dusting brush (a new blusher brush works well)

- cocktail sticks (toothpicks)

- foam block

- foam mat

- bone tool

- quilting tool

- Basic Cake Craft Kit (see Toolbox)

Preparing the cake

1 Trim the crust off the cake with a serrated knife. Place the square cake card on top of the cake and cut around the card, being careful to hold your knife straight and not at an angle (A). Repeat this step to cut out 3 squares of cake.

2 If the squares are not even in height, gently pull a cake leveller through each one to make them uniform (B).

A

B

⌒ A Rose & Lace Romance ⌒

88

3 Use a spatula or palette knife to spread buttercream evenly onto the first layer of cake. Try not to add too much, otherwise it will ooze out of the side of the cake. Add the next layer of cake on top and spread with buttercream as before (C), then top with the final layer of cake.

4 The next stage is to 'crumb coat' the cakes to hold the crumbs of cake in place. First, spread buttercream over the sides of the cakes with the spatula (D).

5 Then spread buttercream over the top of the cake (E). It is easiest to add more buttercream than you need to start with and then scrape off any excess once it has been applied evenly to the whole cake. Aim to spread the buttercream over the cake so that it is thin enough for the crumbs to show through.

6 Place the cake in the fridge until the crumb coat has set (usually about 1 hour). This will make the cake firm so that it is easier to apply the sugarpaste covering (F).

C

D

E

F

⌒ A Rose & Lace Romance ⌒

7   Once the crumb coat has set, knead the pale green sugarpaste well until it is soft and pliable.

8   Using a large non-stick rolling pin, roll out the sugarpaste into a rough square shape on a non-stick board until it is approximately 5mm (³⁄₁₆in) thick. Lift the sugarpaste off the board with the rolling pin and lay it gently over the cake (G).

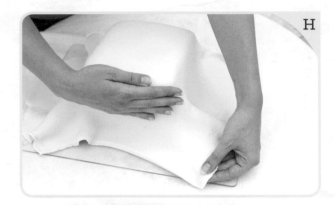

9   Use your hands to smooth the paste over the top and down the corners of the cake. Try to work as quickly as possible to make sure that the sugarpaste doesn't tear on the edges or corners of the cake.

10 Next, use your hands to smooth the sugarpaste over the sides of the cake. As the sugarpaste is smoothed down the sides, you might find that it starts to form pleats towards the base of the cake. If so, gently lift the sugarpaste away from the side of the cake and then smooth it down so that it lays flat against the cake (H). Don't smooth over the top of pleats, otherwise it will leave creases in your sugarpaste.

11 Trim off any excess sugarpaste from around the base of the cake with a small sharp knife.

12 Use a smoother – preferably 2 if you have them – to polish the top and sides (I). This will help press out any air bubbles that may be trapped under the sugarpaste and will give your cake a nice smooth finish.

13 Use a thick brush to dust the sugarpaste covering with edible lustre dust (J).

ᖾ Tip ᖾ

If you get little tears or cracks in your sugarpaste covering, mix a little sugarpaste (same colour as the covering) with water to make slurry (semi-liquid) and gently rub it into the cracks to conceal them.

Stencilled lace pattern

1 Hold the stencil in position on one side of the cake (**A**).

2 Using a spatula, spread an even layer of royal icing across the stencil, making sure that all of the gaps in the stencil are filled (**B**). Be careful not to move the stencil while you are doing this.

3 Carefully lift off the stencil to reveal the lace pattern (**C–D**). Clean the stencil before adding the lace design to each panel of the cake.

4 Attach the cake to the cake board using royal icing. Trim the base of the cake with ribbon, making sure the ribbon is flush with the cake board. Secure with double-sided tape.

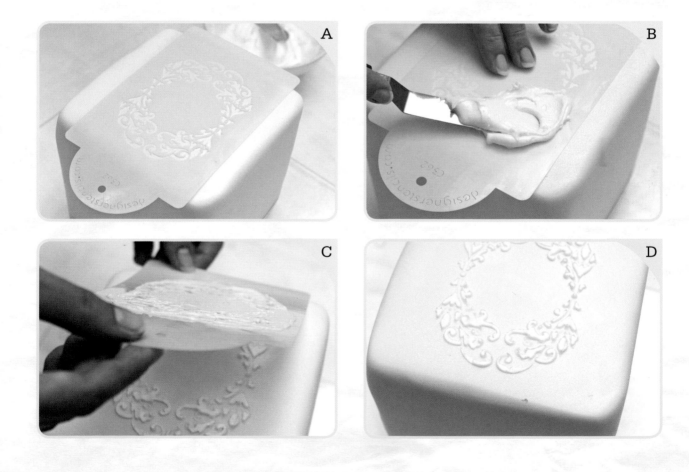

⌒ A Rose & Lace Romance ⌒

Large rose

1 Knead the pale pink flower paste until it is soft. You will know when it is ready to use because it will be stretchy like chewing gum.

2 To make the bud of the rose, roll a small marble-sized ball of the paste into a teardrop and insert a cocktail stick into the base. Make sure that the bud is small enough to fit inside one of the petals of the 5-petal rose cutter. Insert the cocktail stick into a foam block (A).

3 Using a small non-stick rolling pin, roll out the rest of the flower paste thinly on a non-stick board and cut out a flower using the large 5-petal rose cutter (B). Wrap any leftover paste in cling film (plastic wrap) to prevent it from drying out.

4 Place the flower on a foam mat and use a bone tool to gently thin and ruffle the edges of each petal of the flower (C).

5 Turn the flower over gently and use a fine paintbrush to add a little bit of edible glue to the bottom third of each petal (D).

6 Place the flower, glue-side up, on your fingertips, then insert the bud through the centre of the flower. The cocktail stick will be between your fingers and the bud will sit in the middle of the petals. Wrap one petal around the bud; try to wrap it high enough around the top of the bud so that the bud is concealed (E).

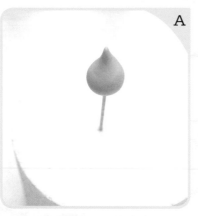

A

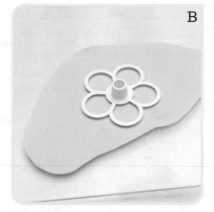

B

C

D

E

7 Take the petal opposite the first petal and wrap it around the bud (**F**).

8 Wrap the last 3 petals around the bud, overlapping each petal as you go (**G**). Use your thumb to gently open out the petals if desired.

9 Place the rose in the foam block (**H**) while you are preparing the next layer of petals, repeating steps 3 and 4.

10 Once you have ruffled the petal edges, turn the flower over carefully on the foam mat and use a cocktail stick to gently curl the edges of each petal (**I**). Turn the flower over again and add glue to the bottom third of each petal.

11 Place the flower, glue-side up, on your fingertips, then insert the rose through the centre of the flower (**J**).

12 Wrap each petal in turn around the rose, overlapping them as you go (**K**). Use your thumb to gently position the petals before leaving the rose to dry (**L**).

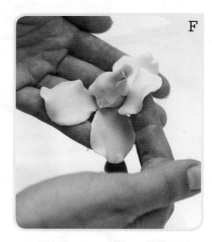

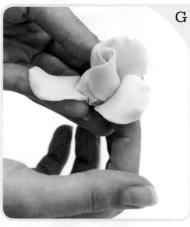

Small roses

1 Roll out the pale pink flower paste thinly on a non-stick board using a non-stick rolling pin and cut out a small flower using the small 5-petal rose cutter.

2 Roll the first petal (petal 1) into a tight cylinder.

3 Wrap petal 3 around the cylinder using a little edible glue if necessary to stick it in place.

4 Next, wrap the remaining petals around the centre petals, overlapping as you go. Start with petal 5, then petal 2 and lastly petal 4, sticking them into position with edible glue. Use your thumb to gently open out the petals.

5 Trim the base of the rose so that it can sit upright on a board, and then leave it to one side to dry. You will need to make 15 roses to decorate the cake, but it is always a good idea to make a few extra ones in case you accidentally drop one!

Rose leaves

1 Roll out the green petal paste thinly on a non-stick board using a non-stick rolling pin and cut out at least 15 small and 2 large leaves using the leaf cutters (A).

2 Use a quilting tool to gently mark along the centre of each leaf (B).

3 Pinch the base of each leaf into a 'V' shape and then leave to one side to dry.

Tip

Make the roses and leaves in advance so that they have dried before adding them to the cake.

Finishing the decoration

Pipe a small amount of royal icing onto the back of each rose and leaf and then stick them into position on the cake. Each panel of the cake should have 3 small roses and 3 small leaves positioned inside the stencilled design. The large rose should be stuck onto the cake board with the base of the rose touching the bottom of the cake, together with 2 large leaves.

Tip

If you find that you have used too much royal icing when attaching the roses and leaves to the cake and the icing is oozing out from behind them, use a dry paintbrush to gently scrape away the excess icing before it sets.

Focus on... HOW TO USE A STENCIL WITH ROYAL ICING

Go to

http://ideas.stitchcraftcreate.co.uk/
kitchen/videos/

for a quick tutorial on how to use royal icing to make a stencilled pattern.

Peony & Pearl Perfection

This gorgeous vintage-inspired cake is decorated with pearls, dainty blossoms and a lovely peony; perfect for a grand, old-time tea party. A range of techniques are encompassed in this project, which will enable you to create a variety of beautiful embellishments and blooms that can also be used for other cake designs and bakes.

TECHNIQUE CHECKLIST *In this project you will learn how to*

- ✓ Cover a round cake with sugarpaste (rolled fondant)
- ✓ Create strands of pearls and a brooch using a silicone mould
- ✓ Use flower (petal/gum) paste to make a peony, small daphnes and leaves
- ✓ Create blossoms using the Mexican hat technique

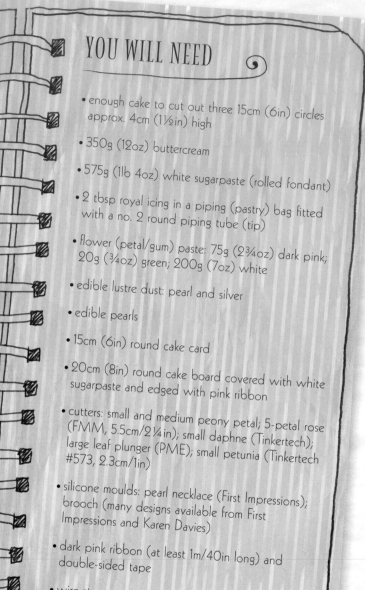

YOU WILL NEED

- enough cake to cut out three 15cm (6in) circles approx. 4cm (1½in) high

- 350g (12oz) buttercream

- 575g (1lb 4oz) white sugarpaste (rolled fondant)

- 2 tbsp royal icing in a piping (pastry) bag fitted with a no. 2 round piping tube (tip)

- flower (petal/gum) paste: 75g (2¾oz) dark pink; 20g (¾oz) green; 200g (7oz) white

- edible lustre dust: pearl and silver

- edible pearls

- 15cm (6in) round cake card

- 20cm (8in) round cake board covered with white sugarpaste and edged with pink ribbon

- cutters: small and medium peony petal; 5-petal rose (FMM, 5.5cm/2¼in); small daphne (Tinkertech); large leaf plunger (PME); small petunia (Tinkertech #573, 2.3cm/1in)

- silicone moulds: pearl necklace (First Impressions); brooch (many designs available from First Impressions and Karen Davies)

- dark pink ribbon (at least 1m/40in long) and double-sided tape

- wire stamens

- bone tool

- foam mat

- ball tool

- small cell stick (or miniature rolling pin)

- Basic Cake Craft Kit (see Toolkit)

Preparing the cake

1 Trim the crust off the cake with a serrated knife. Place the round cake card on top of the cake and cut around the card, being careful to hold your knife straight and not at an angle (A). Repeat to cut out 3 rounds of cake. If the rounds are not even in height, gently pull a cake leveller through each one to make them uniform.

2 Use a spatula or palette knife to spread buttercream evenly onto the first layer of cake (B). Try not to add too much, otherwise it will ooze out of the side of the cake. Add the next layer of cake on top and spread buttercream as before, then top with the final layer of cake.

A

B

~ Peony & Pearl Perfection ~

3 The next stage is to 'crumb coat' the cake to hold the crumbs of cake in place. Spread buttercream over the side and top of the cake with the spatula. It is easiest to add more buttercream than you need to start with and then scrape off any excess once it has been applied evenly to whole cake (C). Aim to spread the buttercream over the cake so that it is thin enough for the crumbs to show through.

4 Place the cake in the fridge until the crumb coat has set (usually about 1 hour). This will make the cake firm so that it is easier to apply the sugarpaste covering.

5 Once the crumb coat has set, knead the white sugarpaste well until it is soft and pliable. Using a large non-stick rolling pin, roll out the sugarpaste in a rough circle shape on a non-stick board until it is approximately 5mm (³⁄₁₆in) thick. Lift the sugarpaste off the board with the rolling pin and lay it gently over the cake (D).

6 Use your hands to smooth the paste over the top and down the side of the cake. Try to work as quickly as possible to make sure that the sugarpaste doesn't tear on the edge of the cake. As the sugarpaste is smoothed down the side, you may find that it starts to form pleats towards the base of the cake. If so, gently lift the sugarpaste away from the side of the cake and smooth it down so that it lays flat against the cake. Don't smooth over the top of pleats, otherwise it will leave creases in your sugarpaste.

7 Trim off any excess sugarpaste from around the base of the cake with a small sharp knife.

8 Use a smoother – preferably 2 if you have them – to polish the top and side of the cake (E). This will help press out any air bubbles that may be trapped under the sugarpaste and will give your cake a nice smooth finish.

9 Attach the cake to the centre of the cake board with royal icing.

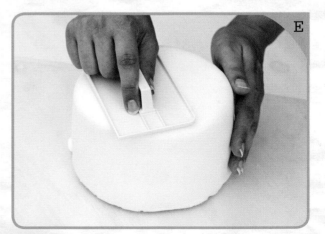

🙎 Peony & Pearl Perfection 🙎

Large peony

1 Roll a ball of dark pink flower paste to approximately 3cm (1¼in) in diameter. Alternatively, you can use a Styrofoam ball if you don't intend the flower to be eaten.

2 Knead the remaining dark pink flower paste until pliable, then use a non-stick rolling pin to roll it out thinly on a non-stick board. Use the small peony cutter to cut out 13 petals, then place them on a foam mat.

3 Use a bone tool to gently frill the edges of the top half of each petal. To achieve very frilly petals the flower paste needs to be very thin. If the bone tool sticks to the petals as you are frilling, you may risk tearing them. If this is the case, leave the petals to dry for a few minutes before frilling again.

4 Using a fine paintbrush, add a small amount of edible glue to the back of 2 petals and attach them, overlapping, on opposite sides over the top of the ball.

5 Add edible glue to the back of 5 petals and arrange them around the ball, overlapping as you go. Be careful not to cover the top of the ball with these petals.

6 Add the last 6 petals as the third layer of the peony, again overlapping them and using edible glue to attach them in place.

~ Peony & Pearl Perfection ~

7 Roll out some more dark pink flower paste and use the medium-sized peony cutter to cut out 7 petals.

8 Use the bone tool to frill the edges of the petals on a foam mat, and then place each petal in a teaspoon to help them dry in a curved shape. Leave the petals to dry for about 30 minutes (they should be leathery in texture but not brittle).

9 Attach the petals to the peony with edible glue, overlapping each one as it is placed in position. Once the petals have been attached, use your fingers to gently arrange them so that they slightly bend towards the flower centre. Place the peony in a glass or small bowl to assist it to dry in a 'cupped' shape overnight.

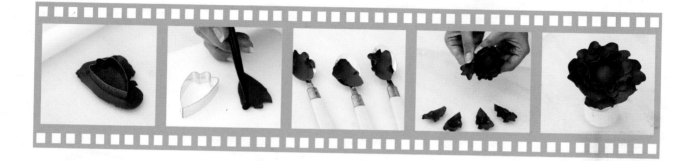

10 Once the peony is dry, repeat steps 7–9 but cut out 9 petals this time, to make the outer layer of the peony.

11 To complete the peony, using a non-stick rolling pin, roll out some green flower paste thinly and use the 5-petal rose cutter to cut out one flower. Wrap the flower around the base of the peony, and secure it in place with edible glue.

12 When the peony is dry, attach it to the top of the cake with royal icing.

Tip

Make the peony first before starting the cake, as it needs to be left to dry overnight.

∽ Peony & Pearl Perfection ∽

strands of pearls

1 Knead the white flower paste until it is soft and pliable. Roll into a thin sausage approximately the length and width of the pearl necklace mould you wish to use.

2 Starting at one end of the mould, press the flower paste firmly along the length of the mould (A). Don't worry if it overfills the mould – just use a knife to trim off the excess paste (B).

3 Flex the mould to remove the pearl strand (C). You will need to make approximately 12 strands of pearls.

4 Using a broad paintbrush, brush each strand with pearl edible lustre dust (D).

5 Starting at the base of the cake, attach each strand of pearls to the side of the cake with a small amount of edible glue applied with a fine paintbrush. If the strands of pearls break as you are attaching them to the cake, simply join them up again with edible glue (E). You will need approximately 1½ strands of pearls for each row.

6 Continue to add rows of pearls until about half of the cake is covered (about 8 rows of pearls). Make sure each row is positioned so that it is touching the previous row and there are no gaps.

7 Attach a dark pink ribbon around the centre of the cake, securing it with double-sided tape so that the bottom edge is flush with the top layer of pearls. You could also add a ribbon bow with long tails to the side of the cake (using double-sided tape).

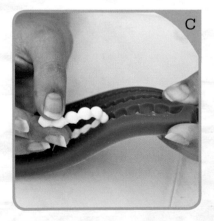

Tip

If you don't have time to make a lot of pearls, you can always modify the design to feature fewer rows of pearls.

Peony & Pearl Perfection

Brooch

1 Knead a small ball of white flowerpaste until it is soft and pliable. Press it into the brooch mould so that the paste is flush with the back of the mould (A). Use a knife to trim off any excess paste if necessary.

2 Flex the mould to carefully remove the brooch.

3 Mix some silver edible lustre dust with clear alcohol or water to make a paint, then apply it to the surface of the brooch with a fine paintbrush (B). Allow the brooch to dry before attaching it to the ribbon bow on the cake with royal icing.

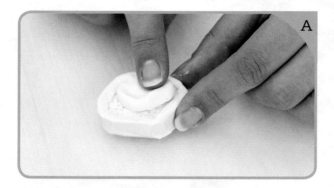

Daphnes and leaves

1 Knead a small ball of white flower paste until it is soft and pliable. Using a small non-stick rolling pin, roll out the flower paste thinly on a non-stick board. Use the small daphne cutter to cut out 5 daphne flowers (A).

2 Place the flowers on a foam mat and then press the small end of a ball tool into the centre of each flower to shape it (B). The more you press down, the more your flowers will form into a cupped shape.

3 Attach an edible pearl to the centre of each flower with royal icing and leave them to dry.

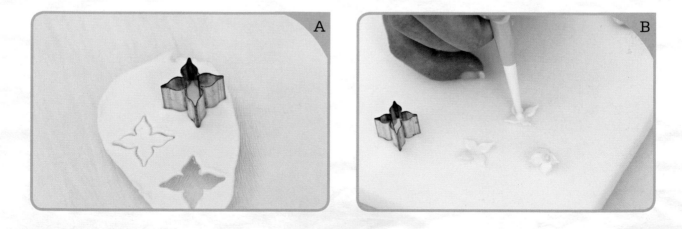

4 To make the leaves, using a small non-stick rolling pin, roll out the green flower paste thinly on a non-stick board. Press the large leaf plunger cutter firmly into the flower paste, and then push down the plunger to imprint veins into the leaf (**C**).

5 Pinch the base of each leaf into a 'V' shape, and then leave to one side to dry (**D**). I have used 6 leaves in my design (4 on top of the cake and 2 on the cake board), but more or less can be added.

6 When the daphnes and leaves are dry, attach to the cake and cake board with royal icing.

Blossoms

1 Knead the white flower paste until it is soft and pliable. Roll a small marble-sized ball of flower paste into a teardrop shape.

2 Pinch around the edge of the teardrop to create a Mexican hat (sombrero) shape.

3 Place the Mexican hat on a non-stick board and use a cell stick (or miniature rolling pin) to thin out the edges of the hat.

Tip

Use a paintbrush to apply edible lustre dust to the edges and centre of the blossoms to add more colour.

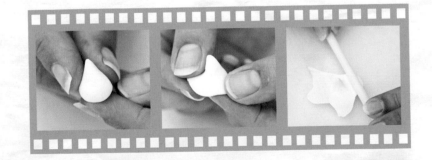

~ Peony & Pearl Perfection ~

4 Place the small petunia cutter over the centre of the Mexican hat and press down firmly to cut out a blossom.

5 Hold the flower in your hands and gently press the cell stick halfway down into the centre of the blossom.

6 Fold 3 strands of fine wire stamens in half and insert into the centre of the flower so that the top of the stamens are sticking out of the blossom. Squeeze the base of the blossom together to secure the stamens in place.

7 Repeat the process to make 5 blossoms.

8 Leave the blossoms to dry before attaching them to the cake with royal icing.

WARNING!

The blossoms that contain wire stamens are not edible, so remember to remove them before serving the cake. Alternatively, you could make them without stamens so that they can be eaten.

Focus on... HOW TO MAKE A BLOSSOM USING THE MEXICAN HAT TECHNIQUE

Go to

http://ideas.stitchcraftcreate.co.uk/kitchen/videos/

for a video tutorial on how to make a blossom with flower paste using the Mexican Hat technique.

❧ Peony & Pearl Perfection ❧

Cake & Cookie Recipes

The following recipes will make a basic sponge cake, cupcake or cookie for you to adapt depending on the size or flavour you want. Tables specify quantities for cakes baked in either round or square tins. It is always useful to bake a cake that is at least 3cm (1¼in) wider than you would like the finished cake to be. This will allow for shrinkage during baking and enable you to remove the crust from the cake without compromising the size. Any cake flavour can be used for the projects in this book. Your imagination is the only limitation!

Easy Peasy (All-in-One) Vanilla Sponge Cake

This is a really handy recipe when you need to make a cake at short notice. It involves minimal preparation and produces a light, fluffy vanilla sponge.

1 Preheat the oven to 180°C/350°F/Gas Mark 4 (160°C/325°F/Gas Mark 3 fan-assisted). Grease the sides and base of the tin (pan) and line the base with baking (parchment) paper.

2 Place all the ingredients (see table) in the bowl of an electric mixer and beat until well blended.

3 Spoon the mixture into the prepared tin and level out with a spatula.

4 Bake in the preheated oven for about 25 minutes, or until well risen, and a skewer inserted in the centre comes out clean. The baking time will be shorter for cakes smaller than 15cm (6in) and longer for cakes larger than 20cm (8in).

5 Remove the cake from the oven but leave it to cool in the tin for at least 5 minutes before turning it out onto a wire rack to cool completely. Don't forget to peel off the baking paper from the base before decorating!

INGREDIENTS

The following quantities will make cakes approximately 7.5cm (3in) deep if they are baked in a single tin (pan). If you don't have a baking tin 7.5cm (3in) deep, divide the mixture between 2 shallower (sandwich) tins at least 4cm (1½in) deep. The mixture will fill about half of the prepared tin and will rise during baking.

Ingredients / Cake Size	7.5 cm (3in) round	10cm (4in) round/7.5cm (3in) square	12.5cm (5in) round/10cm (4in) square	15cm (6in) round/12.5cm (5in) square	18cm (7in) round/15cm (6in) square	20cm (8in) round/18cm (7in) square	23cm (9in) round/20cm (8in) square	25.5cm (10in) round/23cm (9in) square	28cm (11in) round/25.5cm (10in) square	30cm (12in) round/28cm (11in) square
Unsalted butter (room temperature)	30g (1oz)	60g (2¼oz)	75g (2¾oz)	125g (4½oz)	175g (6oz)	225g (8oz)	275g (9½oz)	350g (12oz)	450g (1lb)	575g (1lb 4oz)
Caster (superfine) sugar	30g (1oz)	60g (2¼oz)	75g (2¾oz)	125g (4½oz)	175g (6oz)	225g (8oz)	275g (9½oz)	350g (12oz)	450g (1lb)	575g (1lb 4oz)
Large eggs	1	1	1	2	3	4	5	6	8	10
Self-raising (-rising) flour	30g (1oz)	60g (2¼oz)	75g (2¾oz)	125g (4½oz)	175g (6oz)	225g (8oz)	275g (9½oz)	350g (12oz)	450g (1lb)	575g (1lb 4oz)
Baking powder (tsp)	¼	½	¾	1	1½	2	2½	3	4	5
Vanilla extract (tsp)	½ (2.5ml)	½ (2.5ml)	½ (2.5ml)	¾ (3.75ml)	1 (5ml)	1½ (7.5ml)	1¾ (8.75ml)	2¼ (6.25ml)	3 (15ml)	3¾ (18.75ml)

Adding flavour

Any flavour can be added to your vanilla sponge cake or vanilla cupcakes. Here are some examples:

Lemon Add the juice of ½ a lemon and all the grated zest before adding the flour. There is also a wide range of lemon oils that you can add instead.

Chocolate Replace 70g (2½oz) of the self-raising flour with cocoa powder (unsweetened cocoa).

Coffee Add 3 tbsp (45ml) of espresso (strong coffee) to the mixture.

Super-Quick Chocolate Sponge Cake

This is a lovely chocolate sponge cake recipe. To make it extra decadent, you can use dark cocoa powder or add a liqueur of your choice for an extra kick.

1 Preheat the oven to 180°C/350°F/Gas 4 (160°C/325°F/Gas Mark 3 fan-assisted) and grease and line a baking tin with baking (parchment) paper.

2 Using the ingredient quantities in the table, put the cocoa powder and boiling water into a large bowl and mix well to make a thick paste. Add the remaining ingredients to the bowl and beat with a whisk or large spoon until well combined. This can also be done with electric beaters or in a food processor, but take care not to over-whisk.

3 Spoon the mixture into the prepared baking tin and level out with a spatula.

4 Bake in the preheated oven for about 25–30 minutes, or until well risen. The baking time will be shorter for cakes smaller than 15cm (6in) and longer for cakes larger than 20cm (8in).

5 Remove the cake from the oven but leave it to cool in the tin for at least 5 minutes before turning it out onto a wire rack to cool completely before decorating.

Tip

Avoid taking a sneaky peep at the cake halfway through the baking time – a sudden rush of cool air entering the oven will cause the cake to sink.

Sponge baking knowhow

• Baking tins should be greased and lined to prevent the cake from sticking during baking. To grease the tin, use melted butter or a spray cake release, which should be applied with a pastry brush. To line the base of the tin, cut a circle (for a round tin) or square (for a square tin) of baking (parchment) paper slightly smaller than the diameter/width of the tin. Press into the base of the tin (the paper should stick if you have greased the tin well).

• All ovens are different, so baking times will differ. To check whether cakes are done, they should be firm in the centre and spring back when you touch them lightly with your finger. Another sign that a cake is done is when it starts to shrink away from the sides of the tin.

INGREDIENTS

The following quantities will make cakes approximately 7.5cm (3in) deep if they are baked in a single tin (pan). If you don't have a baking tin 7.5cm (3in) deep, divide the mixture between 2 shallower (sandwich) tins at least 4cm (1½in) deep. The mixture will fill about half of the prepared tin and will rise during baking.

Tip

Chocolate cake tends to have more crumbs than other sponges. Before adding filling or a 'crumb coat', you can use a clean, dry pastry brush to brush off any loose crumbs.

Cake Size / Ingredients	7.5 cm (3in) round	10cm (4in) round/7.5cm (3in) square	12.5cm (5in) round/10cm (4in) square	15cm (6in) round/12.5cm (5in) square	18cm (7in) round/15cm (6in) square	20cm (8in) round/18cm (7in) square	23cm (9in) round/20cm (8in) square	25.5cm (10in) round/23cm (9in) square	28cm (11in) round/25.5cm (10in) square	30cm (12in) round/28cm (11in) square
Cocoa powder (unsweetened cocoa)	10g (¼oz)	15g (½oz)	20g (¾oz)	25g (1oz)	40g (1½oz)	50g (1¾oz)	65g (2½oz)	75g (2¾oz)	100g (3½oz)	125g (4½oz)
Boiling water (tbsp)	¾ (11.25ml)	1½ (22.5ml)	2 (30ml)	3 (45ml)	4½ (67.5ml)	6 (90ml)	7½ (112.5ml)	9 (135ml)	12 (180ml)	15 (225ml)
Unsalted butter (at room temperature)	15g (½oz)	25g (1oz)	35g (1¼oz)	50g (1¾oz)	75g (2¾oz)	100g (3½oz)	125g (4½oz)	150g (5½oz)	200g (7oz)	250g (9oz)
Caster (superfine) sugar	40g (1½oz)	75g (2¾oz)	100g (3½oz)	150g (5½oz)	225g (8oz)	300g (10½oz)	375g (13oz)	450g (1lb)	600g (1lb 5oz)	750g (1lb 10oz)
Large eggs	1	1	1	2	2	3	4	5	6	8
Self-raising (-rising) flour	20g (¾oz)	40g (1½oz)	60g (2¼oz)	90g (3¼oz)	125g (4½oz)	175g (6oz)	225g (8oz)	275g (9½oz)	350g (12oz)	425g (15oz)
Baking powder (tsp)	⅛	¼	⅓	½	¾	1	1¼	1½	2	2½
Full-fat (whole) milk (tbsp)	½ (7.5ml)	1 (15ml)	1⅓ (20ml)	2 (30ml)	3 (45ml)	4 (60ml)	5 (75ml)	6 (90ml)	8 (120ml)	10 (150ml)

Cake & Cookie Recipes

Vanilla Cupcakes

This is a basic vanilla cupcake recipe that never fails to produce domed fluffy cupcakes, ready to decorate as you desire.

INGREDIENTS

Makes 12 large (muffin-sized) cupcakes or 16 small cupcakes (fairy cakes)

- 175g (6oz) unsalted butter, at room temperature
- 175g (6oz) caster (superfine) sugar
- 3 large eggs, at room temperature
- 1 tsp (5ml) vanilla extract
- 175g (6oz) self-raising (-rising) flour

1 Preheat the oven to 180°C/350°F/Gas Mark 4 (160°C/325°F/Gas Mark 3 fan-assisted). Line a cupcake baking tray (pan) with cupcake cases (liners).

2 While the oven is heating up, use an electric mixer to beat the butter and sugar together until the mixture lightens in colour (this will take about 5 minutes) and has a mousse-like texture.

3 Gradually add the eggs to the mixture, and ensure that they are mixed in well after each addition. Beat in the vanilla extract. Sift the flour into the mixture and stir carefully with a spoon until all the ingredients are combined.

4 Spoon the mixture into the cupcake cases until they are about two-thirds full. Bake the cupcakes in the preheated oven for about 20 minutes until their tops are slightly golden or until a skewer inserted into the centre of one of the cupcakes comes out clean.

5 After removing from the oven, leave the cupcakes to cool for about 5 minutes in the tin before transferring them to a wire rack to cool completely before decorating.

Cupcake knowhow

- Using eggs and butter at room temperature will make baking easier. Leave the butter out of the fridge for about an hour and it will be soft enough to beat together with the sugar to achieve a pale, fluffy mixture. Cold eggs can cause the mixture to curdle. If this happens, you can rescue the mixture by vigorously whisking in a large tablespoon of flour.

- Store cupcakes in a cardboard cupcake box or a loosely sealed (not airtight) container for up to 3 days. They may sweat and come out of their paper cases (liners) if stored in an airtight container and air cannot circulate around them.

All about cupcake cases

Cupcake cases (liners) come in a wide variety of sizes and colours, and are made from a range of materials. Some paper cases are sturdier than others, so it is best to try different types for yourself and see which you prefer. All cupcake cases (except silicone and cardboard cases) need to be placed in a cupcake baking tray (pan) before the cupcake mixture is added, as they are generally not robust enough to hold their shape during baking without support.

• **Paper cases** These regular cases have not been made with greaseproof or glassine paper, so often the butter from the cupcake may bleed through the case and cause greasy marks on the paper. To help prevent this, try using 2 paper cases instead of one.

• **Greaseproof cases** These cases are made from paper that has been refined until it is not very porous. This stops liquids and butter from being able to penetrate the case.

• **Glassine paper cases** These cases are similar to greaseproof ones, and stop grease from seeping through. Glassine paper is treated with steam during the manufacturing process, giving it a shiny surface.

• **Foil cases** These cases are very sturdy and the grease from the cupcake mixture will not seep through. Gold and silver foil cases are the most popular, but other colours can be found as well.

• **Silicone cases** These cases do not need to be placed in a cupcake baking tray and can be baked on a flat baking (cookie) sheet. They can also be washed and reused, but because they not disposable, they may not be ideal to use for cupcakes you have made as a gift, as you may not get your cases back!

• **Cardboard cases** These cases can be placed directly on a flat baking (cookie) sheet. They come in a range of lovely patterns, making them perfect to present cupcakes that have been baked as a special gift.

• **Cupcake wraps** These paper or cardboard wraps are placed around a cupcake after it has been baked in a case and cooled. They come in a variety of patterns and colours and help dress up your cupcake and give it a professional finish. Most wraps are not greaseproof, so it's a good idea to wait to add them to the cupcakes just before they are served, to prevent grease spots appearing on them.

Tip

Cupcake case (liner) sizes are not standardized, so be sure to check that your cases fit in your cupcake baking tray (pan) before making your cupcake mixture.

US cup measurements

If you prefer to use US cup measurements, please use the following conversions.
(Note: 1 Australian tbsp = 20ml.)

LIQUID
1 tsp = 5ml
1 tbsp = 15ml
½ cup = 120ml (4fl oz)
1 cup = 240ml (8½fl oz)

BUTTER
½ cup/1 stick = 115g (4oz)
1 cup/2 sticks = 225g (8oz)

CASTER (SUPERFINE) SUGAR
½ cup = 100g (3½oz)
1 cup = 200g (7oz)

**ICING (CONFECTIONERS')
SUGAR, UNSIFTED**
1 cup = 115g (4oz)

**PLAIN (ALL-PURPOSE) AND
SELF-RAISING (-RISING) FLOUR**
1 cup = 125g (4½oz)

**COCOA POWDER
(UNSWEETENED COCOA)**
1 cup = 100g (3½oz)

Vanilla Cookies

A lot of cookie recipes I have used in the past make cookies that spread
during baking. This recipe, however, makes cookies that will hold their shape.
Like most cookie doughs, it also freezes well for at least a month, so you can
wrap half of it in cling film (plastic wrap) and save it for another day.

INGREDIENTS

Makes 30 large cookies

• 175g (6oz) unsalted butter,
at room temperature

• 200g (7oz) caster (superfine) sugar

• 2 large eggs (room temperature)

• 1 tsp (5ml) vanilla extract

• 400g (14oz) plain (all-purpose) flour

• ½ tsp salt

1 Using an electric mixer, beat the butter and sugar together until pale and fluffy. Then beat in the eggs one at a time, followed by the vanilla extract.

2 In another bowl, combine the flour and salt. Add to the butter and egg mixture and mix gently until well combined. You will probably find that the electric mixer struggles to combine all the ingredients once the flour and salt are added, so you may have to mix it all together with a spoon.

3 Form the dough into a flattened disc and wrap it in cling film (plastic wrap) or a plastic bag before placing it in the fridge for at least an hour to firm up.

4 While the dough is in the fridge, preheat the oven to 180°C/350°F/Gas Mark 4 (160°C/325°F/Gas Mark 3 fan-assisted).

5 Once the dough is ready to roll out, sprinkle a wooden board (or another work surface) with flour, place the dough on it and roll it out to about 6mm (¼in) thick. If you find that the dough sticks to the rolling pin, place a piece of cling film (plastic wrap) or baking (parchment) paper between the dough and the rolling pin. You can also add a little bit of flour to the dough if it is really sticky, but do so sparingly, as too much flour will make the dough tough.

6 Using cookie cutters or a knife, cut the dough into shapes. Use a spatula to carefully lift the cookies onto baking trays (sheets) lined with baking paper, making sure you allow some space between them so that they aren't touching.

7 Bake the cookies in the preheated oven for 8–12 minutes. You will know when they are ready when the edges just start turning gold. Don't worry if they are still soft in the centre – they will firm up as they cool. Use a spatula to transfer the cookies to a wire rack to cool. Wait until they have completely cooled before decorating.

Cookie knowhow

• Try to make sure that all the cookies on a baking tray (sheet) are approximately the same size to allow for an even bake.

• Bear in mind that larger cookies take longer to bake than smaller ones.

• To achieve cookies that are all the same thickness, roll out the dough between spacers.

• Food colourings can be added to cookie dough before it is rolled out and baked, to make coloured cookies!

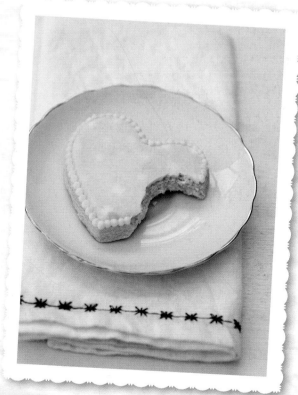

Fillings

Buttercream and ganache are two of the most popular fillings for cakes. They can also be used to 'crumb coat' (seal) a cake before it is covered with sugarpaste (rolled fondant). The following recipes for these fillings can be flavoured to your own requirements.

Vanilla Buttercream

This classic light, fluffy filling is simply made by beating together butter and icing (confectioners') sugar.

INGREDIENTS

Makes about 500g (1lb 2oz), enough to fill and 'crumb coat' a 20cm (8in) cake with 3 layers, or 24 cupcakes

- 175g (9oz) unsalted butter, at room temperature

- 350g (12oz) icing (confectioners') sugar, sifted

- 2 tbsp (30ml) cooled boiled water

- 1 tsp (5ml) vanilla extract

1 Using an electric mixer, beat all the ingredients together for at least 5 minutes until the mixture is pale and fluffy. It is best to start mixing on slow speed to prevent the icing sugar from covering the kitchen and then gradually build up to a fast speed.

2 Any other flavourings or colourings can also then be mixed into the buttercream.

Tip

Buttercream can be stored in an airtight container in the fridge for up to 1 week. Remove it from the fridge at least 30 minutes before it is needed, to bring it to room temperature.

Buttercream knowhow

• Buttercream will always be slightly yellow in colour due to its butter content. This is tricky to counteract, especially if you are trying to colour it pink, as it generally turns an apricot colour when pink or red food colourings are added. A whitening agent (Superwhite) from cake decorating suppliers can fix this problem. White buttercream can also be made if white vegetable fat (shortening) is added instead of butter.

• Cover the mixing bowl with a damp clean tea (dish) towel while mixing the buttercream to stop the icing sugar from escaping!

• To thin the buttercream, add water, a little at a time, until the desired consistency is achieved.

• If your kitchen is particularly warm, it may help to add a pinch of cream of tartar to your buttercream to help it firm up.

Ganache

Ganache is a mixture of melted chocolate and cream. It can be poured over cakes while still warm as a glaze, or it can be cooled and beaten to achieve a spreadable consistency — perfect for filling and covering cakes. Ganache can be stored in the fridge for about 2 weeks, or frozen for up to 3 months. Allow the ganache to stand at room temperature to soften before use.

INGREDIENTS

Makes enough dark, milk or white chocolate ganache to fill and cover a 20cm (8in) cake with 3 layers

• 125ml (4fl oz) double (heavy) cream

• 200g (7oz) dark (bittersweet) chocolate or milk chocolate or 360g (12½oz) white chocolate, broken into small pieces

1 Bring the cream to the boil in a small saucepan.

2 Remove the saucepan from the heat and stir in the chocolate until smooth.

3 Allow the mixture to cool to room temperature (if not being used as a glaze) before beating with an electric mixer or spoon to the desired consistency.

Ganache knowhow

White chocolate can be a bit tricky to work with, as it can split (become grainy) if it is overheated. Adding more white chocolate in proportion to the amount of cream (as compared with milk or dark chocolate) will help to overcome this problem.

Icings

Sugarpaste, flower paste and royal icing will help you transform your cakes into works of art, and are essential for making a wide range of decorations. Both sugarpaste and flower paste can be bought in a range of colours from cake decorating stores or online suppliers, while royal icing is easily made and coloured as you need it.

Sugarpaste

Sugarpaste (also known as rolled fondant, plastic icing or ready-to-roll icing) is a sugar dough used to cover cakes and make edible decorations. It has a relatively long shelf life and is readily available in supermarkets and cake decorating supply stores in a range of colours. If you prefer not to use a commercial sugarpaste, you can make your own using the following recipe.

INGREDIENTS

Makes 500g (1lb 2oz) white sugarpaste

- 500g (1lb 2oz) icing (confectioners') sugar, plus extra for dusting

- 2 tbsp (30ml) liquid glucose

- 1 large egg white

1 Sift the icing sugar into a large bowl. Make a well in the centre and slowly stir in the liquid glucose and egg white with a wooden spoon until the mixture is combined into a dough.

2 Place the sugarpaste on a surface dusted with icing sugar and knead until smooth and pliable. You may need to sprinkle the sugarpaste with extra icing sugar if it becomes too sticky. The sugarpaste can be used immediately or wrapped tightly in cling film (plastic wrap) and stored until required.

Tip

Sugarpaste can be mixed in a ratio of 50:50 with flower paste to make a more pliable but still durable modelling paste, which is useful for creating sugar models and drapes.

Marshmallow Sugarpaste

Sugarpaste can also be made with marshmallows, which is known as marshmallow sugarpaste (fondant). Some people prefer using this type of sugarpaste because it is softer and sweeter than regular sugarpaste.

INGREDIENTS

Makes 500g (1lb 2oz) white marshmallow sugarpaste

- 500g (1lb 2oz) white mini marshmallows

- 2 tbsp (30ml) water

- white vegetable fat (shortening), for greasing

- 575g (1lb 4oz) icing (confectioners') sugar, sifted

1 Place the mini marshmallows and water in a large microwave-proof bowl and then place the bowl in a microwave for 1 minute on a medium setting. Allow the mixture to rest for 1 minute, then microwave it again for another minute.

2 Remove the bowl from the microwave and then stir the mixture with a wooden spoon that has been greased with white vegetable fat (to stop the mixture sticking to it) until smooth.

3 Stir in the icing sugar until well combined.

4 Knead the marshmallow sugarpaste until smooth. Wrap it in cling film (plastic wrap) and store at room temperature until required.

Tip

Marshmallow sugarpaste is softer than regular sugarpaste, so it may be more challenging to use when covering cakes.

Sugarpaste knowhow

- Don't store a sugarpaste-covered cake in the fridge, as the icing or decorations are likely to absorb condensation and will wilt.

- It's best to store a cake covered with sugarpaste in a cardboard box, not an airtight container, so that air can circulate around it. Otherwise, the sugarpaste will sweat and the decorations may become soft.

- Sugarpaste is too soft for making delicate decorations, but adding gum tragacanth (1 tsp to 250g/9oz sugarpaste) will give it more strength and then it can be rolled more thinly.

- If your sugarpaste becomes dry while you are working with it, white vegetable fat (shortening) can be kneaded into it to soften it.

- Sugarpaste will keep well for months if it is tightly wrapped in cling film (plastic wrap) and stored at room temperature.

Estimating sugarpaste quantities

The following illustrations provide an estimate of the amount of sugarpaste you will need to cover round and square cakes. It is always wise to use a bit more sugarpaste than specified (trim off the excess and store it for future use) if you are not very experienced at covering cakes. The quantities given assume that the sugarpaste is rolled out to about 5–6mm (¼in) thick.

ROUND CAKE SIZE (DIAMETER)

SUGARPASTE QUANTITIES

	7.5cm (3in) high	10cm (4in) high
10cm (4in)	285g (10oz)	400g (14oz)
15cm (6in)	400g (14oz)	500g (1lb 2oz)
20cm (8in)	500g (1lb 2oz)	680g (1lb 8oz)
25.5cm (10in)	680g (1lb 8oz)	1kg (2lb 4oz)
30cm (12in)	1kg (2lb 4oz)	1.4kg (3lb 1oz)

SQUARE CAKE SIZE (WIDTH)

SUGARPASTE QUANTITIES

	10cm (4in) high
10cm (4in)	500g (1lb 2oz)
15cm (6in)	680g (1lb 8oz)
20cm (8in)	1kg (2lb 4oz)
25.5cm (10in)	1.4kg (3lb 1oz)
30cm (12in)	2kg (4lb 8oz)

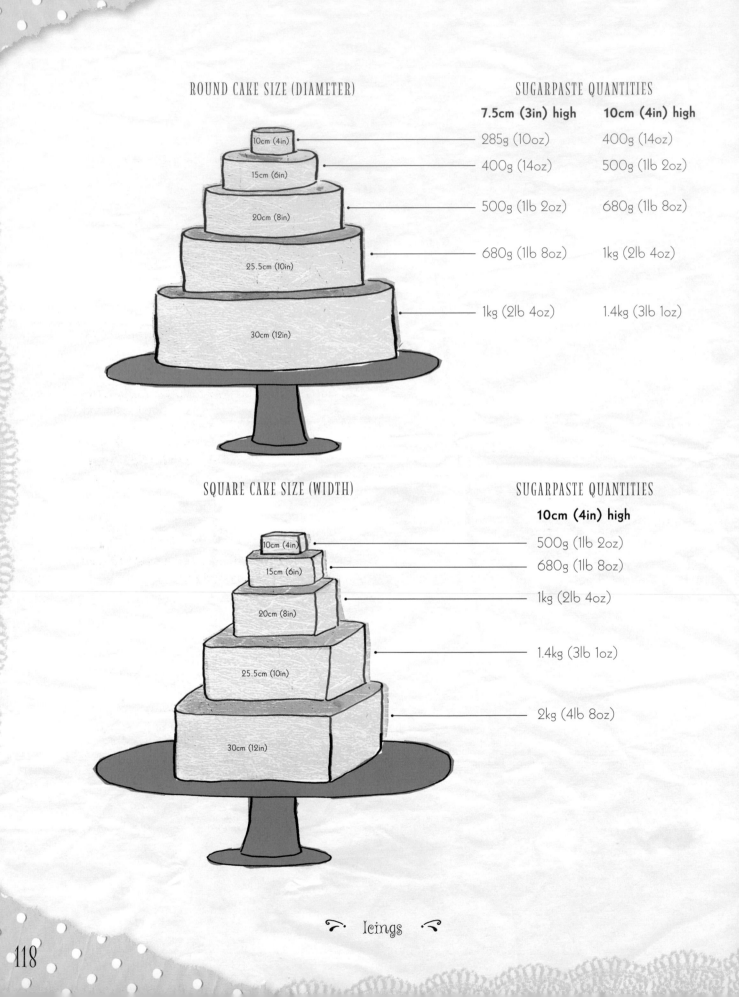

◦⌒◦ Icings ◦⌒◦

Flower Paste

Flower paste (also known as petal, gum or sugar florist paste) is a sugarpaste dough that contains a gum-stiffening agent. It is often used for making flowers and intricate decorations because it can be rolled paper thin without breaking and gives a smooth but tough finish. Flower paste is susceptible to heat and humidity, and should be wrapped tightly in cling film (plastic wrap) and stored in an airtight container when not in use.

INGREDIENTS

Makes approx. 900g (2lb) white flower paste

- 4 large egg whites
- 900g (2lb) icing (confectioners') sugar, plus extra for dusting
- 12 tsp tylose powder
- 4 tsp white vegetable fat (shortening)

1 Place the egg whites in the bowl of an electric mixer and mix on high speed for 10 seconds to break up the egg whites.

2 Turn the mixer to the lowest speed and slowly add 800g (1lb 12oz) of the icing sugar. This will make a soft-peak royal icing.

3 Once the icing sugar has combined with the egg whites, turn the mixer to a medium speed and mix for another 2 minutes.

4 Turn the mixer to the slow setting and mix in the tylose powder. You will notice that the mixture will begin to thicken.

5 Scrape the mixture out of the bowl onto a work surface that has been sprinkled with icing sugar. Grease your hands with the white vegetable fat and then knead the flower paste, adding the remaining 100g (3½oz) of the icing sugar to form a soft, smooth dough. To check that you have kneaded your flower paste enough, your fingers should come away clean after pinching the paste.

6 Wrap the flower paste well in cling film (plastic wrap) and place in the fridge for 24 hours if possible before use. Allow the flower paste to come to room temperature before using.

Tip

Gum tragacanth can be used instead of tylose powder to make flower paste. However, tylose powder is generally less expensive and makes a whiter flower paste.

Colouring sugarpaste and flower paste

Liquid food colourings are not suitable for colouring sugarpaste (rolled fondant) or flower (petal/gum) paste because they change the consistency of the paste, making it sticky and difficult to work with. It is best to use gel (concentrated) colourings and add the colouring gradually until the desired colour is achieved.

1 Use a cocktail stick (toothpick) to add the colouring to the paste. Darker colours will need more colouring than lighter shades.

2 Knead well until an even colour is achieved.

Tip

To prevent your hands from being dyed when colouring paste, it is advisable to wear disposable gloves.

Using dust and glitter

Official food safety classifications in relation to lustre dust and glitter have recently been changed and you should check these products to determine whether they have been deemed 'edible', 'for food contact' or 'non-toxic', and follow the manufacturer's instructions for use accordingly. Only dust or glitter clearly labelled as 'edible' should be applied to food for consumption. All other dusts and glitters are intended for decoration purposes only – to be used on decorations that are to be removed and not eaten. If you are unsure if a non-toxic dust or glitter is safe for use in contact with food, you should contact the dust or glitter supplier.

Instead of using glitter, there are many other commercially available edible decorations to add sparkle to your cakes:

Nonpareils Also known as hundreds and thousands, these tiny sugar balls are available in many colours.
Dragées These are small sugar balls with an edible metallic coating. Those with an iridescent coating are often called edible pearls.
Sprinkles Also known as jimmies, these small rod-shaped pieces of chocolate come in a wide range of colours.
Sanding sugar These transparent sugar crystals are available in many different colours.

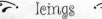

Royal Icing

Royal icing is a mixture of icing (confectioners') sugar and egg white that sets firm. The icing can be thinned (made softer) by mixing in small amounts of water. Stiff-peak royal icing (which is not thinned with water) is used for piping delicate decorations such as flowers, and for attaching decorations to cakes. Medium and soft-peak royal icing are often used for piping intricate designs, and the icing can be thinned down to a liquid to 'flood' (fill in) cookies. Royal icing can also be coloured using gel or liquid food colourings.

INGREDIENTS

Makes 250g (9oz) stiff-peak royal icing

- 240g (8½oz) icing (confectioners') sugar

- 1 large egg white

- ¼ teaspoon lemon juice

1 Sift the icing sugar into the mixing bowl of an electric mixer and add the egg white.

2 Mix together on low speed for about 5 minutes until the icing has a stiff-peak consistency.

3 Mix in the lemon juice with a wooden spoon.

Tip

Dried egg white or meringue powder mixed with water can be used instead of fresh egg white to make royal icing. Raw eggs should not be used in food prepared for pregnant women, young children or anyone whose health is compromised.

Royal icing knowhow

- It is important to keep royal icing away from the air, as it dries out quickly and will develop a crust on its surface that will make it unsuitable for piping — the crust will block the piping tube (tip). To prevent a crust from forming, cover freshly made royal icing with cling film (plastic wrap) and then a damp cloth.

- Royal icing can be stored for up to 5 days in an airtight container in the fridge. Re-mix it with a wooden spoon when it is needed to achieve the desired consistency.

- When piping royal icing, how stiff you want to make the icing is a personal choice, but as a rule, if the icing dribbles out of the tube by itself, it's too soft. Conversely, if you can't pipe without squeezing the bag so hard that it is likely to split, then it's too stiff. A medium consistency is always a good starting point.

Presentation

After taking your time to decorate your cake to perfection, it is important to display it in its best light. Here are a few tips to help you make your cake a true showstopper.

Covering a cake board with sugarpaste

Give your cake a professional finish by placing it on a cake board covered with sugarpaste.

1 Knead sugarpaste on a non-stick board until it is smooth and pliable.

2 Using a non-stick rolling pin, roll out the sugarpaste to approximately 4mm (⅛in) thick.

3 Dampen the cake board with a moistened cloth, then lift the sugarpaste over the rolling pin, roll it over the top of the cake board and use your hands to smooth it down over the board (A).

4 Cut off the excess sugarpaste with a knife (B).

5 Use a smoother, if you have one, or the palm of your hand to polish the surface of the paste.

6 Rub a finger around the rim of the cake board to smooth the edges.

Trimming a cake board with ribbon

Once a cake board has been covered with sugarpaste, a length of ribbon 1.5cm (⅝in) wide can be attached around the edge of the board using double-sided tape (A).

A

Tip

Use a coloured ribbon on the edge of the cake board that matches or complements the cake design.

Cake stands

There are oodles of cake stands and serving plates available to suit all cake types. It is important to choose a stand that can support the weight of the cake and that enhances the cake's design. As a general rule, the width of your cake should be 2.5–5cm (1–2in) smaller than the plate it rests on.

Tip

Adding an appropriately coloured ribbon to the cake stand can also help tie it into the cake design.

Suppliers

UK
CAKE SUPPLIES

Alphabet Moulds
www.alphabetmoulds.co.uk
16 Winston Road, Barry,
Vale of Glamorgan CF62 9SW
Tel: 0144 642 0901

Cakeology Ltd
www.cakeology.net
582 Kingston Road,
London SW20 8DN
Tel: 0208 127 5166

Cakes, Cookies and Crafts Shop
www.cakescookiesandcraftsshop.
co.uk
Unit 2 Francis Business Park,
White Lund Industrial Estate,
Morecambe, Lancashire LA3 3PT
Tel: 0152 438 9684

Cake Decorating Company
www.thecakedecoratingcompany.
co.uk
Unit 2b Triumph Road,
Nottingham NG7 2GA
Tel: 0115 969 9800

Cake Stuff
www.cake-stuff.com
Units 1–5, Gateside Industrial
Estate,
Lesmahagow, Lanarkshire,
Scotland ML11 0JR
Tel: 0155 589 0111

Fine Cut Sugarcraft Shop
www.finecutsugarcraft.com
Workshop 4, Old Stable Block,
Holme Pierrepont Hall,
Holme Pierrepont,
Nottingham NG12 2LD
Tel: 0115 933 4349

Karen Davies Sugarcraft Ltd
www.karendaviescakes.co.uk
Unit 4, Royal Standard House,
330–334 New Chester Road,
Birkenhead, Merseyside CH42 1LE
Tel: 0151 643 0055

Knightsbridge PME Ltd
www.cakedecoration.co.uk
Unit 21, Riverwalk Road,
Enfield EN3 7QN
Tel: 0203 234 0049

Lindy's Cakes Ltd
www.lindyscakes.co.uk
Unit 2, Station Approach,
Wendover, Aylesbury,
Buckinghamshire HP22 6BN
Tel: 0129 662 2418

Squires Kitchen Shop
www.squires-shop.com
3 Waverly Lane, Farnham,
Surrey GU9 8BB
Tel: 0845 617 1810

Stitch Craft Create
www.stitchcraftcreate.co.uk
Brunel House, Newton Abbot,
Devon TQ12 4PU
Tel: 0844 880 5852

CAKE STANDS AND
PRESENTATION SUPPLIES

Nicholas & Steele
www.nicholasandsteele.co.uk
78 Durham Road,
West Wimbledon,
London SW20 0TL
Tel: 0794 701 1879

VV Rouleaux
www.vvrouleaux.com
5 Western Bank, Wigton,
Cumbria CA7 9SJ
Tel: 0207 224 5179

US

Designer Stencils
www.designerstencils.com
2503 Silverside Road,
Wilmington, DE 19810
Tel: 800-822-7836

Fancy Flours
www.fancyflours.com
705 Osterman Drive, Suite E,
Bozeman, MT 59715
Tel: 406-587-0118

Global Sugar Art
www.globalsugarart.com
625 Route 3, Unit 3,
Plattsburgh, NY 12901
Tel: 800-420-6088

Australia

Cake Deco
www.cakedeco.com.au
Shop 7, Port Phillip Arcade,
232 Flinders Street,
Melbourne, Victoria
Tel: 03 9654 5335

Cakes Around Town
www.cakesaroundtown.com.au
Unit 2/12 Sudbury Street,
Darra, Brisbane QLD 4076
Tel: 07 3160 8728

Cake Decorating Solutions
www.cakedecoratingsolutions.com.au
Shop 7A, 69 Holbeche Road,
Arndell Park, NSW 2148
Tel: 02 9676 2032

About the Author

Fiona started cake decorating as a hobby in 2009 when she moved to London from Sydney. While completing training in cake decorating at Brooklands College, her cake designs became predominantly inspired by the vintage era and she found her passion lay in creating small baked treats such as cupcakes, cookies and small celebration cakes, and teaching others how to make them.

After winning a number of awards for her cupcakes, Fiona's pretty bakes grew in demand, allowing her to set up her business — Icing Bliss — in 2011. She also regularly teaches classes at Cakeology Ltd in South West London.

www.icingbliss.co.uk
www.facebook.com/icingbliss

Acknowledgments

I have thoroughly enjoyed writing this book and would like to thank everyone who has helped to make *Cake Craft Made Easy* possible. It has been a great team effort and I could not have done it without the help of the following people:

Many thanks to my publisher and the team at David & Charles — James Brooks, Victoria Marks and Grace Harvey, and to my project editor Jo Richardson — for their wealth of great advice and support in creating this book. A huge thank you also to my wonderful photographer Sian Irvine and her assistants who worked incredibly hard to capture all of the cakes and the steps to present them in their best light. A big thank you as well to James Mabbett and Vince North from Webvid for putting the video tutorials together. It has been wonderful working with you all.

I am so grateful to have been supported by my friends, family and the wonderful online baking community during the preparation of this book. A special thanks also to my friends and colleagues at Cakeology Ltd for all of their encouragement and suggestions.

Finally, and most importantly, a huge amount of gratitude goes to my husband Dave for his endless support and patience, and for his honest critique of all of my trials and errors. This book wouldn't have been possible without you — thanks for always being my biggest fan!

Index

A DAVID & CHARLES BOOK
© F&W Media International, LTD 2013

David & Charles is an imprint of F&W Media International, LTD
Brunel House, Forde Close, Newton Abbot, TQ12 4PU, UK

F&W Media International, LTD is a subsidiary of F+W Media, Inc.
4700 East Galbraith Road, Cincinnati, OH 45236

First published in the UK and USA in 2013
Digital edition published in 2013

Text and designs © Fiona Pearce 2013
Layout and photography © F&W Media International, LTD 2013

Fiona Pearce has asserted her right to be identified as author of this work in
accordance with the Copyright, Designs and Patents Act, 1988.

A catalogue record for this book is available from the
British Library.

ISBN-13: 978-1-4463-0291-0 paperback
ISBN-10: 1-4463-0291-1 paperback

Paperback edition printed in China by RR Donnelley
for F&W Media International, LTD
Brunel House, Forde Close, Newton Abbot, TQ12 4PU, UK

10 9 8 7 6 5 4 3 2 1

Publisher: Alison Myer
Junior Acquisitions Editor: James Brooks
Project Editor: Jo Richardson
Senior Designer: Victoria Marks
Photographer: Sian Irvine
Videographers: James Mabett and Vince North
Production Manager: Bev Richardson

F+W Media, Inc. publishes high-quality books on a wide
range of subjects. For more great book ideas visit:
www.stitchcraftcreate.co.uk